Foreword

I am delighted to welcome this exhibition, *Masterpieces of Serbian Goldsmiths' Work* to the Victoria and Albert Museum. It has come to us as part of a cultural exchange between England and Yugoslavia, and I hope that it will be as successful as the exhibition of English silver sent out from the V&A to Belgrade and Zagreb last year. It will certainly expose the English public to many fine and rare objects, some from the inaccessible treasuries of Serbian monasteries, and will give us a glimpse of the art produced by this ancient state, influenced first by the Byzantines and then by the Turks, but also absorbing forms and decoration from the West.

ROY STRONG
Director, Victoria and Albert Museum

Introduction

By Bojana Radojković

In September 1980 a notable exhibition of English Silver was held in Belgrade at the Museum of Applied Art. It was a very attractive display: experts from the Victoria and Albert Museum, who organized the exhibition, succeeded in presenting our public with the development of English silver from the fifteenth century to the end of the second decade of the twentieth century.

Now the Belgrade Museum of Applied Art is privileged to bring the work of Serbian craftsmen to London. The exhibition contains objects ranging from the thirteenth to the eighteenth century.

Displayed are earrings, bracelets, rings, and diadems, as well as Church silver, chalices, cups, crosses and reliquaries. Also included are heavy silver-gilt vessels which were often described as of gold; consequently, in Serbian terminology the craftsman working in silver is called a goldsmith.

The development of Serbian craftsmanship in silver was long and idiosyncratic, and this is reflected in the objects displayed in the exhibition. In fact the craft developed in much the same way as did the mediaeval Serbian state, but when the Serbian state ceased to exist after the assaults of Turkish invaders in the fifteenth century, the craft of the silversmith lived on and continued developing, with new artistic impulses coming from Turkey. Although there were no longer the powerful domestic feudal lords to commission silver and gold vessels and jewellery, there was still the Church which, even under Turkish domination, was able to commission precious Gospel covers, reliquaries in architectural forms and valuable chalices, thanks to the people's donations.

Sixteenth-century travellers give astonished accounts of the splendour of the churches in Serbia and this has enabled us to trace the development of Serbian silverwork even after the Serbian state no longer existed. This development reflects the oscillations and vicissitudes in the life of the Serbian people, the

1

new trends in art which appeared, and then disappeared, and the old styles which after long centuries resurfaced as echoes of a distant past.

When the Serbs, together with other Slavic tribes, came to the Balkan Peninsula in the seventh century, they found the great culture of the Byzantine Empire whose roots were Greco-Roman in origin. By the mid-tenth century the Serbs had expanded their power over the inland of the Balkan Peninsula as far as the Field of Kosovo, but their economy still rested on primitive agriculture and cattle raising, while the political power was in the hands of their tribal chiefs. In the middle of the ninth century, Serbia as a region of the Balkan inland became an obstacle to the expanding Bulgaria. To neutralise the Bulgarian conquests, lest they should expand farther towards its territory, the Byzantine Empire turned to the Balkan countries and gave assistance to the Serbs. By converting them to Christianity around 874 AD, it opened up many opportunities for exerting Byzantine influence.

In the territory between Bulgaria to the east, and Hungary to the north, a Serbian state was growing gradually. During the eleventh and twelfth centuries, the Byzantine Empire was ruled by the powerful Comnenus dynasty, and thus Serbia could not manage to gain independence. But Stefan Nemanja (1170–1196), the Grand Head of the tribal state of Ras and founder of the Nemanjić dynasty, succeeded after Manual Comnenus's death in expanding the Serbian state and finally achieving its independence; but for fear of his main rivals in the Balkans, Bulgaria and Hungary, he still turned to the Byzantine Empire for support. During his reign the influence of Byzantine culture on Serbia was especially strong. Following the example of the Byzantine Empire and its rulers, Nemanja built monasteries which were to become the backbone of cultural life for the Serbs, and were the places where books were transcribed, literacy and education promoted, and workshops founded to satisfy the monastic needs; it was in these workshops that goldsmiths also worked. Nemanja was a very wise ruler, capable of harmonizing his policy between East and West. The two Churches, the Catholic and Eastern Orthodox co-existed in Serbia, and Nemanja supported both of them: the churches and monasteries he erected were Eastern Orthodox, and yet he used to send valuable presents to Rome, to the Church of Saints Peter and Paul, and to the Basilica of Saint Nicholas in Bari. Nemanja also built Hilandar monastery (the monastery of Chilendari) on Mount Athos and bestowed upon it the silver liturgical vessels manufactured in the workshops at his monastery, Studenica, in Serbia. Nemanja's sons, Stefan Prvovenčani (Stefan the First Crowned) and

Sava wrote their father's biography in which they described the valuable presents which Nemanja had donated to churches, and extolled his deeds.

During his reign, Nemanja made his younger son, Stefan (1196–1227), heir to the throne, married him to a Byzantine princess, and then went to Mt. Athos where he entered the monastic order for the rest of his life. After his father's death, Stefan fought briefly with his elder brother Vukan whom Nemanja, in fear of the Hungarian influence because of his marriage to a Hungarian princess, a relative of Pope Innocent III (1198–1216), had deprived of his right to the throne. Stefan overcame his brother and succeeded in consolidating his position on the Serbian throne. Then he broke up his marriage with the Byzantine princess and wedded the Venetian, Anna Dandolo, who brought with her some Venetian goldsmiths.

At that time the Crusaders crushed the Byzantine Empire and founded the Latin Empire (1204), the Thessalonian kingdom and other Crusader states, leaving only the smaller Byzantine states in the Balkans and Asia Minor. All this led to the strengthening of Serbia. To enhance his fame, Stefan decided to be crowned king, and he received his crown from Pope Honorius III in 1217. The King's brother, Sava, as a monk and abbot of Studenica monastery, the pious endowment of his father, went to the East, to Nicaea, where the Patriarch granted him permission to found the Serbian autocephalic, (that is, independent) Church, with Sava as its first archbishop. All these events of course had their effect on the development of art and the crafts in Serbia: the domestic goldsmiths were now making articles which imitated Byzantine art; some goldsmiths' work with Romanesque-Gothic characteristics was coming from Hungary; the Mediterranean and especially Apulian influences were reflected in the goldsmiths' work from the Dalmatian coast, particularly from Bar, Kotor and Dubrovnik. Serbian crosses, reliquaries and jewellery of this time have certain characteristics which distinguish them from both Eastern and Western goldsmiths' work: the cloak buckles are adorned with decorative motifs of Romanesque-Gothic origin, and tiny palmettes intertwined with figures of fantastic animals and griffons. This ornamentation is similar to the stone carving found on the church of Bogorodična (Mother of Jesus) at Studenica and shows that already in the late twelfth and early thirteenth century a characteristic style prevailed in the decorative arts of Serbia.

The thirteenth century saw a period of great prosperity. The first flowering of literature took place and the economic situation made it possible for painting to evolve freely (as at the monasteries of Mileševa and Sopocáni), and the gold-smiths' craft developed most richly. At the Mt. Athos monastery of Chilendari (Hilandar), built by Nemanja and Sava, monks collected books, translated from the Greek into the Serbian, and also wrote original works, while the same activity was taking place in other monasteries elsewhere.

Stefan Prvovenčani's sons, King Radoslav (1227–1234) and King Vladislav (1234–1243), were not the equals of their father and grandfather as politicians, but they were great patrons of art. King Radoslav's mother and wife were both Greek, and his sympathies and artistic interests were directed towards Byzantium. King Vladislav, on the other hand, was married to a Hungarian princess and, during his reign, the German miners (the Saxons, called *Sassi* in Serbia), fleeing before the Tartar invasion, migrated from Hungary to Serbia and began exploiting the Serbian mines. Thus King Vladislav became the first Serbian ruler to mint coins. Together with his brother Radoslav, he built Mileševa Monastery to which he moved the relics of his uncle Sava, who had been proclaimed a Serbian saint, and thus the cult of St. Sava was created there. Sava's silver-gilt coffin was decorated with embossed pictorial plaques which attracted great attention from contemporaries. The quantity as well as quality of goldsmiths' work being produced was high, as shown by the inventory of the valuable objects which Beloslava, King Vladislav's wife, together with her son, placed for safekeeping in Dubrovnik. This inventory, now in the Historical Archives of Dubrovnik, shows that they owned large Gospels in gold covers decorated with precious stones and enamel, crosses and reliquaries mounted in silver, old silver icons 'left by our predecessors', luxurious belts, silver and gold cups, and many other valuables such as were found in almost every noble house of the period, not just at the ruler's court. This detailed inventory reflects a standard of living which modelled itself on the luxury of the Byzantine emperors, and, like other archival source material, fills in the large gaps between the very small number of actual surviving pieces.

Stefan Prvovenčani's third son, Uroš (1243–1276) was lucky enough to be able to encourage economic prosperity in his country. The exploitation of the mines, particularly of the silver, gold, lead and copper mines was increased. Markets sprang up around the mining centres attracting merchandise from many parts of the country and, at the same time, ores, wrought, and unwrought metals were bought and sold. Where there were markets, there also were goldsmiths' shops with Serbian craftsmen. These were the origins of the future urban goldsmiths who would eventually have special privileges in comparison with other craftsmen of that time.

According to the surviving charters dating from the thirteenth century, which were sent to monasteries and churches, there were also goldsmiths on the feudal estates and thanks to these records we can see how they lived there. When a ruler endowed a church with some property, such as villages, forests and the like, he also mentioned in his charter the goldsmiths who lived in the endowed villages. They were treated as free serfs but were obliged to make one part of their products for the monastery, while the rest they were allowed to sell. Potters, wood-carvers and tailors bound to a feudal estate enjoyed the same treatment, but continually to deal in his craft, the craftsman had to teach his eldest son the same trade. However, besides these partially free craftsmen on the feudal estates, there were also goldsmith-serfs, that is, those who were not free to dispose of their products. Goldsmiths' shops were also growing up in Serbian towns and cities, but the craftsmen who ran them were free citizens who could dispose of their property as they liked; they owned houses and shops of their own, and they employed apprentices from other parts to learn the trade; often they were rich men. Goldsmiths from the Adriatic Coast, particularly those from Kotor and Dubrovnik, visited Serbian inland towns, sold their goldware and established new workshops there.

King Uroš was married to Jelena Curtié, a close relation of the Neapolitan house of Anjou. Being French-born and Catholic, she built and supported both Catholic and Eastern Orthodox churches. For her pious endowment, the Monastery of Gradac, she ordered a gold cross with fragments of the Holy Cross which cost an enormous sum of money. King Uroš donated gold pectorals to his archbishop, while he himself wore around his neck a precious gold cross set with costly gems. In addition to these luxurious articles, Serbian goldsmiths made small-size silver reliquaries decorated with sculptural figures of Holy Warriors, the Virgin Mary with Jesus Christ, and the Holy Fathers. At the same time, they manufactured secular silver-gilt vessels with inscriptions and decorative motifs on them.

Jewellery was also made: rings with decorative niello inlay, earrings of the thin filigree wire, diadems composed of tiny silver tablets, and so on. In its decorative motifs and shapes, Serbian goldsmiths' work of the thirteenth century reflects first of all Byzantine influences; it combines these with Gothic elements however: the Gothic rosette and S-shaped motifs, beside typically Byzantine tiny vine tendrils, and the ivy leaf together with palmettes. By the second half of the fourteenth century these Eastern and Western motifs had fused homogeneously and idiosyncratically.

The sources of ornament which the Serbian goldsmith could draw on were varied: they were the designs in illuminated manuscripts, in church frescoes and in eastern and western fabrics.

Thirteenth-century Serbian illuminated manuscripts display ornament which is closely linked to Byzantine and oriental art as well as related to Apulian art which, in turn, uses Byzantine motifs in late Romanesque and early Gothic colouring. As these manuscripts circulated freely from one part of the country to another, their ornament was easily accessible as models to all craftsmen, and above all to goldsmiths. The ornamentation found in the wall-painting of churches was also an immense treasury of design from which craftsmen could gather models. Throughout the Middles Ages, Serbia imported textiles from both East and West: Archbishop Sava bought in the East valuable fabrics woven with the figures of eagles, lions and fantastic animals. His brother, Stefan Prvovenčani, and later, Kings Vladislav and Uroš, also imported luxurious fabrics from Italy, via Venice; and thus the richly decorated materials, interwoven with gold thread, made in Ancona, Venice, Lucca, Padova and Genoa and other Mediterranean centres were reaching the Serbian feudal courts and markets together with the cloth of Flanders and distant England. Thus the rich ornamental repertory found in imported textiles also influenced the craft of the Serbian goldsmith. During the second half of the 13th century Serbian goldsmiths' work also echoes the shapes of imported western articles from Limoges, Westphalia and Central Europe.

We can only get an inkling of the richness and luxury of the courts of the Serbian rulers in this and the next century. Niciphore Gregoras, who in his writings speaks of the Serbian court with much irony and malice, cannot get over the impression of crude luxury. But perhaps that crudeness, so often emphasized by the Byzantine envoys when speaking about life at Nemanjić's court, just denoted a special style of clothing, and, particularly, of jewellery, which shared the characteristics of Central European and Italian personal ornaments, and which also seemed barbaric to the aristocratic orthodox Byzantines.

The reign of King Milutin (1282–1321), the second son of King Uroš, saw the conquest of new territories, the building of big churches and monasteries in Serbia and elsewhere, the growth of mining and the flourishing of crafts, especially the craft of the goldsmith: substantial quantities of silver were exported from Serbia to the Republic of Dubrovnik, and expensive fabrics and jewellery imported. Dubrovnik conducted negotiations with Venice about the eventual coming of the well-known Venetian goldsmith Peter to King Milutin's court in order to make various articles for him. Milutin's marriage to the Byzantine, Princess Simonida, in the late 13th century further increased the luxury of the Serbian court and nobility. Theodore Metokhit, the Byzantine envoy who had negotiated the royal match, could not help being impressed by the splendour he saw there, accustomed as he was to splendour and luxury back home. He writes about the precious jewellery that adorned King Milutin, about the banquet at which venison and other roast meats were served on gold and silver plates, about the precious cups of gold and silver, and forks and spoons with gold and silver handles. As the luxury increased after Simonida's wedding, the malicious Greeks now said that they were afraid that all the wealth of the Byzantine imperial treasury would be shifted to Serbia, so that Empress Eirene could curry favour with her son-in-law, the mighty king who was expanding his kingdom towards the north and south.

However, here again very little of this has survived to the present day: a few rings, bracelets, and silver-gilt cups; but fortunately the surviving frescoes showing Serbian rulers conjure up the splendour of King Milutin's court.

After the King's death, battles for the throne were fought, and Milutin's son, Stefan Dečanski (1322–1331), came out victorious. However, his reign was not long for he was dethroned by his son Dušan with the help of the Serbian feudal lords.

The reign of Czar Dušan (1331–1355) was marked by conquests which finally brought the boundaries of the Serbian state as far as the Aegean Sea. Serbia became an empire, the Church was raised to the level of a Patriarchate, and Dušan's Legal Code proclaimed. This incorporated the Byzantine legal codes, including the articles pertaining to goldsmiths. The development of the arts, particularly the goldsmith's craft, continued and was to bring about the forma-tion of a singular homogeneous style which survived throughout the fourteenth century. But this reign also had its dark side which became apparent immedi-ately after Dušan's death: Dušan had favoured the feudal lords who, in their lust for conquests, had helped him to power before his father's death. By granting them large parcels of every newly conquered land, Dušan had made them into powerful landed gentry.

During the reign of his young son, Czar Uroš (1355–1371), the feudal lords took control over some regions and only nominally recognized the supreme power of the Czar. The Serbian mines were no longer in the possession of the Czar as an absolute ruler but fell into the hands of the nobles who leased them out to a variety of people, most often the wealthy entrepreneurs of Dubrovnik. The exploitation of the Serbian mines, particularly the silver mines, went as far as it could, which, of course, made it possible for the powerful feudal lords to amass money quickly which they spent only partly on defence and mercenaries, while the bulk they kept for themselves and their luxurious life. Thus disunited, the Serbian state was jeopardized by the invasion of the Turks who were gradually conquering the southern parts of the Balkan Peninsula. In the battle of Marica (on the River Maritsa) the Serbian regional lords tried to hinder the Turkish advance but failed, and the Turks were victorious. The second fateful clash with the Ottomans, the battle of Kosovo, took place in 1389, but the

Serbian army was routed again, and one of the most important feudal lords, the Grand Duke Lazar, was killed in the battle. After that, only three feudal regions, the Lazarević's, Branković's and Balšić's, remained of what was once a powerful empire. The Grand Duke Lazar's son, Stefan Lazarević (1380–1427) united all three regions into one, thus creating a unified state under the supreme power of the Turks. Stefan Lazarević, as a Turkish vassal, took part in the battle of Angola, in 1402, and, after the Turkish defeat, got the title of Serbian Despot from the Ottomans in Constantinople. Now turning to Hungary, he got the region of Mačva and Belgrade which became his seat. Despite the Turkish devastation of Serbia, the economic conditions, thanks to the mines, quickly improved and the country faced a brighter prospect. As a Despot's demesne, Serbia was quickly recovering after the fall, and now a brilliant art form evolved, which was essentially linked with the times of King Milutin and Czar Dušan. Never before were all Serbia's arts to closely linked into one style as from the 1370s right down to the fall of the Despot's demesne (1459). Just as Serbian painting experienced a new flowering, so did the craft of the goldsmith. The jewellery with its refined shapes and decorative motifs, the silver-gilt plate with engraved ornamentation, the luxurious resplendent crosses and reliquaries with their religious compositions – all speak of the prosperity which prevailed at that time. From the records kept in the Dubrovnik Archives, we also learn how Serbian goldsmiths lived during Dušan's reign until the fall of the Despot's demesne. To give just one example: the goldsmith Pribil appears in a document as the guarantor for the grand feudal lord Djordje Balšić (1377) which means that the economic power of some Serbian goldsmiths was almost equal to that of the feudal lords.

During Serbia's battles with the Turks many a great feudal lord had taken his property into the monasteries Dubrovnik and Mt. Athos. The lists of these deposits have survived to this day, and they tell us what the gentry possessed and kept at their courts. In addition to jewellery – gold earrings with precious stones, particularly emeralds – there were gilt cups with engraved monograms and coats of arms decorated with enamel. Besides the cups, there were valuable plates, face- and handwashing utensils, icons set in silver, Gospels in precious settings, and many other valuables. One Bosnian noble even owned a musical instrument, a portable organ.

The style of this period is called the Moravska (after the Morava river), and it consists of interlacing ornament combined with figures of fantastic animals, naturalistically swelling leaves, and flowers of an indefinably oriental sort with double palmettes and fine elegant figures in relief.

The nephew and successor of Stefan Lazarević, Djuradj Branković, the last Despot of free Serbia, also cherished the goldsmiths' trade. When he acquired the relics of St. Luke, he decreed that a silver coffin should be made to protect them during the transport from Epirus to his seat, Smederevo, in Serbia. This silver coffin must have been very luxurious, because Empress Mara, Djuradj's daughter and Sultan Murat II's wife, presented precious textiles as an extra adornment for it, and Djuradj paid 30,000 ducats for the relics alone, or so said his grand daughter, Jelena, ten years later when she offered the coffin for sale to the Doge of Venice.

But in 1459 the Serbian state fell completely into Turkish hands, and many branches of art either faded away or vegetated under the difficult living conditions, the goldsmiths' craft, however, continuing to exist. Serbia's gold-smiths, well-off people, together with a certain number of the landed gentry, crossed the boundaries, the Sava and Danube rivers, and settled down in what was then Southern Hungary (today's Vojvodina). In some centres where the Turks had not yet arrived, goldsmiths' shops were opened; one of the biggest being in Bečkerek (Zrenjanin). The Serbian goldsmiths Petar Smederevac whose name tells us that he came from Smederevo in Serbia , Vuk and Djordje Gostimirović, and many others worked here. It is worth emphasizing that their products were mostly commissioned by clergy who tried to fill the newly built churches in this region with ecclesiastical silver. Thus, in 1559 Petar Smederevac set in silver the Gospel that belonged to the Eastern Orthodox bishop Vladika Maksim Branković, former Serbian Despot turned monk. This Gospel setting, to be seen in this exhibition (cat. no. 95), shows very clearly the skill and great artistic powers of the old Serbian goldsmiths. The expressive qualities of its iconography surpass those of average goldsmiths' work. At the same time, the goldsmith Dmitar of Lipova (1550–51) made for the monastery of Sišatovac a reliquary which has a very interesting shape and decorative motifs (cat. no. 105). It is in the form of a five-domed church with a portal representing the Annunciation, while the sides of the nave are decorated with half-figures of the Apostles, the Prophets, the fathers of the Church, and Serbian saints. Decorative vines of Arabic origin and motifs whose style can be associated with the Gothic alternate on the drums of the enzola.

Dmitar of Lipova did not only work for the monastery of Sišatovac: a similar, almost identical *artophorion* is in the monastery of St Catherine, in the Sinai Peninsula, but we have no idea how it arrived there. Indeed, the works of many Serbian masters are scattered all over the world, for, owing to difficult economic conditions, many churches were forced to pawn or even sell parts of their treasuries, and many were looted during the Balkan wars.

In the parts of the country under the Turks, Serbian silversmiths continued to make many liturgical vessels for the local Church, particularly after the Renovation of the Patriarchate of Peć (1559). Thus the goldsmith Kondo Vuk, commissioned by Radivoje who is thought to have been one of the Christian *spakhias* (landowners), made a wood-mounted silver icon (the so-called *ripida* icon with a handle) for the monastery of Dečani which had been looted after the battle of Kosovo (1389).

After the arrival of the Turks, the feudal lords who had submitted to Turkish power and fought on the Turkish side remained on their own feudal estates and continued in their own religion. Because the Turks had no hereditary aristocracy, but every common Turkish soldier could become a *spakhia* if he excelled in the battle, so some Christian feudal lords who fought on the Turkish side, were allowed to keep their estates, and to support their own Church. At the sixteenth-century Sultan's court there were even some Serbs, converts to Islam, who held high office, such as Mehemet-Pasha Sokolović, the Grand Vizier of Suleiman the Magnificent. Mehemet-Pasha Sokolović's brother, a Serbian monk, used his brother's influence to renew the Patriarchate of Peć and, eventually, to become Patriarch of Serbia himself. This led to Turkish permission being granted for the renovation of churches and monasteries, and even for the construction of new ones.

At the monastery of Banja, near Priboj on the River Lim, Yugoslav archaeologists have recently excavated part of this monastery's treasury which had been hidden under the altar floor by some unknown monk to hide it from the advancing Turks. All the objects date from the sixteenth and seventeenth centuries, after the renovation of the Patriarchate of Peć, and they all represent high quality work by Serbian craftsmen. There were many such objects in all churches throughout Serbia as testified to by the travellers from the west who passed through these parts in the sixteenth and seventeenth centuries, and who mention the appalling difference between the churches full of resplendent gold and silver articles, and the poor population hiding in dugouts.

It is interesting to analyse the style of these sixteenth-century articles. The Gospel covers are adorned with sculptural images of the saints and with decorative motifs. The wood-mounted silver icons with handles (*ripidas*) are embossed and engraved with liturgical compositions. Figures are predominant here while ornament fills the empty spaces and plays a secondary role. The personalities represented are individualised, their bodies being lightly and skilfully modelled, while the composition and the order of the figures follows the old Byzantine schemes. The reliquary-*artophorions* in architectural form with three or five domes imitate contemporary churches. The long inscriptions found on them refer both to the pious citizens who donated money and to the learned monks who devised the iconographical schemes in compliance with Church rules and regulations. The silver cups, which also had their specific ritual significance, are decorated with portraits of the apostles and saints, and with compositions linked to their liturgical use. The crosses are set in luxurious filigree mountings and adorned with enamel. The pectoral pendants, chests and smaller reliquaries for keeping small-size wooden icons, are also in silver and decorated with figures of saints, scenes from the life of Jesus Christ or ornamental motifs. Gilding has a special role here: some parts of an object, when gilt, especially gilt reliefs, assume purely colouristic effects, and thus the entire relief attains a sculptural quality, as though inspired by painting.

What is particularly interesting once again is the stylistic marriage between oriental and western influences. Until Serbia's fall into Turkish hands, it was Byzantine art from the East combined with Romanesque-Gothic motifs coming from the West that had influenced the Serbians; but in the Turkish period, in the sixteenth century, Islamic-Turkish motifs were also arriving from the East, while of the western styles it was Gothic motifs which continued to prevail. What conspicuously distinguishes sixteenth-century Serbian silverwork from that of the other Balkan countries is the sculptural figures which are not hard, static and lifeless, but fluid, expressive and direct, representing themes such as the Ascension, the Resurrection, the Nativity, the Death of the Virgin, and her Assumption.

Sixteenth-century Serbian silversmiths scarcely had the opportunity to show their skill at making secular articles, and therefore they never felt the influence of the Renaissance which in Italy was already turning into Mannerism – there were no patrons to further this – but they did continue to work for the Church. They made Church plate and vessels of ritual significance, with decoration which comprises interlacing animals, fantastic monsters and human figures; these figures are full of movement, and are set in a design of decorative vines, chick-pea leaves and double palmettes borrowed from the old Byzantine as well as Turco-Persian arts. As a final touch to the compositions Gothic cross-shaped leaflets, which survive from an earlier period, also appear.

Indeed, in the 1580s, perhaps for lack of new decorative motifs, the Gothic style resurfaces in the objects made by Serbian silversmiths and survives as late as the 1660s. This retardataire Gothic, is not, however, part of figurative compositions but influences the form and ornament of objects.

For example, earlier, in the mid-fourteenth century, Serbian craftsmen had made bronze censers under Gothic influence, but the moulds for them had come from Central European workshops. The manufacture of censers went on also during the sixteenth century, but now they were in silver, with Serbian inscriptions, and were considerably richer than the old ones. Being composed of biforms, triforms, and with pinnacles and pilasters, these censers are reminiscent of the architecture of Gothic churches. The origin of this delayed, ornate, flowery Gothic can be found in the coastal area, along the Dalmation coast which, through its craftsmen and merchants, was closely connected with the inland where the 'flowery' Gothic also existed in the sixteenth century. In Walachia and Moldavia, both Christian Orthodox countries free from the Turks, where many Serbian silversmiths had found refuge, the Gothic style was still cherished under the influence of Transylvania. But while the Gothic had died out there by the early 17th century, with the Serbs under the Turks it survived until long after the Baroque had prevailed in the neighbouring countries. It is almost as though Serbian craftsmen were disassociating themselves from Islamic art and trying to import something western, something Christian, regardless of the fact that it was old and long forgotten. Thus Gothic motifs appeared during the seventeenth century on reliquary – *artophorions*, censers, crosses and many other articles which had never been decorated in this way before. Gothic decorative elements were to oust the figurative compositions and, side by side with the Islamic ornamental motifs, to dominate the craft.

Also in the sixteenth century, the engraving of silver book covers developed under the influence of Serbian incunabula and graphic arts. The fine and light drawing found here is somewhat reminiscent of figures conceived in the Renaissance manner. This is explained to some extent by the fact that in the first half of the sixteenth century, Božidar Vuković of Podgorica (Montenegro) had run his printing shop in Venice, from which books in Cyrillic had been arriving in the Turkish Balkans. One could say that this printing shop's ornamentation, engravings and compositions served as a manual for Serbian silversmiths.

Then, in the seventeenth century, engraving and sculptural reliefs gradually disappeared, giving way more and more frequently to individual cast figures which were combined to make a composition on the book cover. The relief compositions by some silversmiths of the seventeenth century, such as, for example, those by Neško Prolimleković of Požarevac (cat. no. 100), look fresh in their naive expressiveness, but they foreshadow the decay of the art form: thus ornament ousts the figures and the figures themselves gradually become ornament.

The second half of the seventeenth, and especially the late seventeenth century, saw the gradual disappearance of those pseudo-Gothic motifs as well, and Islamic ornament took its place instead. By the beginning of the eighteenth century, a variant of the Baroque finally came to the Balkans, and also to Serbia. This was mixed with Islamic motifs which led to the formation of the so-called Levantine Baroque. Figures and figurative compositions disappeared, and the decorative motifs were now composed of cartouches, spirals, stylized acanthus leaves mixed with chick-pea stems, and arabesques. Church vessels and reliquaries, however, were still dominated by the old pseudo-Byzantine style which was exceptionally clearly reflected in the large reliquary – *artophorions*. Daskal Stefan, a pious monk who had come from the Serbian monastery of Ravanica to the newly erected Ravanica in Srem, Vojvodina, ordered from the goldsmith, Nikola Nedeljković, a large reliquary-*artophorion* in the form of the old Ravanica Monastery (cat. no. 111). Master Nikola composed in low relief on the outer walls of its nave a work in the spirit of the ancient art, representing figures of the Serbian ruler-saints, Stefan Nemanja, King Milutin, and the Grand Duke Lazar, the ruler-Martyr who had been killed in the battle of Kosovo fighting the Turks. The other walls of this monumental goldsmith's work he adorned with green and blue enamel.

This is one of the last great works of old Serbian goldsmiths' work, which, during the eighteenth century gradually lost its freshness and declined into using misunderstood and often repeated motifs without life or beauty. The stylistic battle was lost, not so much because of difficult economic conditions but because the Russian Baroque was coming from the East, and western Baroque from Europe, so strangling the old Byzantine art forms in the Balkans.

There was one branch of the goldsmith's craft, however, which went on living – jewellery. In the first years of Turkish occupation jewellery had been made of silver-plated tin and non-precious metals decorated with various small coins and pendants. Earrings after the old models, rings with new decorative motifs, and chest and head jewellery composed of silver chainlets were still manufactured under the influence of Turkey. Necklaces, in time, became ever bulkier, and were adorned with decorative motifs of Islamic origin. Semiprecious stones – agate and carnelian – played a more and more important role in jewellery, especially in the late seventeenth and throughout the eighteenth century. Belts were specially adorned, because right from the Middle Ages, the belt had had a significant symbolic function. In Dušan's Legal Code (1349) mentioned earlier, the belt is referred to as a token of the feudal nobility, and this is why it had to be richly decorated. This luxurious belt ornamentation persisted in Serbia right down to the eighteenth century. The sixteenth-century belts were made of silver gilt and were decorated with filigree. The seventeenth-century belts are composed of flower-like and snake-like silver medallions, and also of large cut carnelians and agates, to luxurious effect. Belts with agates and carnelians arranged in the form of a cross in varying shades ranging from deep brown to light brown produce an extraordinary richness of colour. Serbian silversmiths thus tried to give a special freshness to their jewellery, relying, of course, on the materials they could acquire.

The Austrian-Turkish wars in the late seventeenth century caused great confusion in the Serbian crafts. Battles, and the arrival of the Austrian army, the Turkish attacks, the repeated pressing of the Austrians across the Danube and Sava rivers, and the Great Migration of the Serbs across the same river in 1690 were not propitious for any development of goldsmiths' trade. The eighteenth century saw permanent unrest, and the early nineteenth, the struggle of the Serbian people for their liberation from the Turks. The First Serbian Uprising, in 1804, which was crushed in blood and gore in 1813, the Second Serbian Uprising in 1815, and the final liberation from the Turks, directed Serbian craftsmen towards the Western European countries, particularly towards Vienna, Budapest and, finally, Paris. The manufactured silver articles and gold jewellery brought from abroad completely ousted the ancient goldsmiths' craft and the goldsmiths tried gradually to learn and grasp the new styles coming from Western Europe. So died an important branch of ancient Serbian art.

Catalogue

By Dušan Milovanović

Illustrated by catalogue number

3

1 Ring
Late 12th, early 13th century
Cast silver; chased
Height: 24 mm   Width: 22 mm
Archaeological find from Lešje (tomb No. 37), Serbia.

The cross-section of the hoop is rectangular and widens towards the bezel; the shoulders of the ring are decorated with chased linear ornament.

The round bezel is engraved with two birds standing by the Tree of Life. These reveal the hand of a domestic craftsman, and Romanesque influence.

12th and 13th century Serbian silversmiths were strongly inspired by motifs found in the designs of textiles imported from Italy.

Inv. No. 3929, National Museum, Belgrade
Literature: B. Radojković, *Jewellery in Serbia,* (Belgrade 1969) pp. 109–110.

2 Ring
Circa 1380
Cast silver; engraved, enamelled
Height: 27 mm   Width: 22mm
Find from the surroundings of Novi Pazar, Serbia.

In the form of an ellipse drawn towards the bezel; semicircular in section and profiled. The elongated shoulders of the ring widen towards the elliptical bezel. The hoop bears linear ornament once filled with green enamel. The engraving on the bezel represents a lion passant with a star on one paw.

Lions often appear in Moravska Serbian ornament on coins (cf the Smederevo Despot's dinars), wall decoration, textiles, heraldry, and jewellery.

The models for rings of this type were Gothic silver articles from Italy brought to Serbia by silversmiths of Kotor and Dubrovnik.

Inv. No. 698, Museum of Applied Art, Belgrade
Literature: B. Radojković, (1969) p. 197.

3 Ring
End of 14th century
Cast silver; chased; set with an intaglio
Height: 34 mm   Width: 30 mm
Found at Novo Brdo, Serbia.

A heavy round hoop, semicircular in section, widens towards the shoulders and forms a massive elliptical bezel. The hoop is ornamented with engraved palmettes, semi-palmettes and fern leaves. One strip of ornament around the ring's shoulders consists of straight lines, and the other of Gothic, heart-shaped zigzag lines. These motifs first went from Byzantium to influence Italian goldsmiths' work in the high Romanesque period, and then were imported to Serbia from Italy. An antique intaglio with the figure of Nike is set in the centre of the bezel. The inscription around the gem reads, 'This ring belongs to Radule', an unidentified Serbian feudal lord.

Made in a workshop at Novo Brdo where a large number of similar rings was found.

Inv. No. 4407, Museum of Applied Art, Belgrade
Literature: B. Radojković, (1969) pp. 173–174.

4 Ring
End of 14th century
Cast silver; chased, silver-gilt niello
Height: 31 mm   Width: 20 mm
Found at Novo Brdo, Serbia.

A round hoop, triangular in section, profiled, widens towards the ring's shoulders. Decorated with two strips of stylized plant ornament filled with niello. The hoop gradually rises towards the ring's shoulders, chased with a design of broken branchlets.

The bezel is round and protruding and encircled by a sinuous vine.

The flat surface of the bezel is engraved with a standing figure of an eagle with half displayed wings.

Archaeological Institute of the Serbian Academy of Sciences and Arts (SANU), Belgrade
Literature: B. Radojković, (1969) p. 172.

5 Ring
Second half of 14th or early 15th century
Cast gold; chased, engraved
Height: 24 mm   Width: 22 mm
Found near Janjevo, Serbia.
Signet Ring.

An elliptical hoop elongated towards the octagonal bezel and engraved with a coat-of-arms and inscription. The narrowest part of the band bears an inscription in two hardly legible lines; the first line reads, 'memento . . . me'; the second, 'discipula tua Domino.' On the band, above the inscription, are engraved heptagonal stars in circles with frames in the form of a deltoid. The shoulders are chased with closed lilies and branchlets on the sides.

The bezel is deeply engraved with a wolf's head and the letter 'P'. Around it is inscribed, 'annelo de peto' ('the secret ring'). Although closely resembling Italian rings of that time, it was probably made by a local craftsman. The large number of the surviving similar rings reflect European influence in Serbia.

Inv. No. 4949, Museum of Applied Art, Belgrade
Literature: B. Radojković, (1969) pp. 197–200.

6 Ring
Late 14th or early 15th century
Wrought silver; chased
Height: 20 mm   Width of the bezel: 18 mm
Found in Kosovo, Serbia.

A semicircular band, rectangular in sections, widens slightly towards the bezel. The hoop is engraved with shield-shaped linear ornament. The bezel is round and flat; two lines are engraved around it while a monster with spread wings, scales all over its body, and big claws is in the middle.

Rings of this type are closely related to the decorative stone sculpture of the Moravska School (the late 14th to the first half of the 15th century) by contemporary literature.

Inv. No. 4428, Museum of Applied Art, Belgrade
Literature: B. Radojković, (1969) pp. 188, 194.

7

5

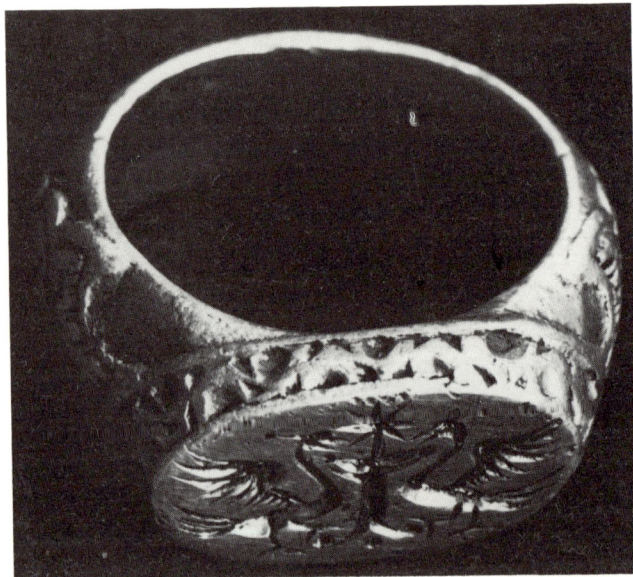

7 Ring
Early 15th century
Cast silver; chased
Width: 19 mm
Found in the surroundings of Peć.

Cast in one piece. The bezel is round, semicircular in section, with a widened portion on its narrow shoulders. The shoulders are decorated with stylized palmettes, with heart-shaped leaves and strips of stylized leaflets.

In Serbian ornament these motifs are found in the frescoes at the Monasteries of Sveto Nagoričane, St. Sofia of Okhrid, Bogoridica (Our Lady) Ljeviška, and Dečani. The decoration on this ring, however, is functionally reduced and its ornament is therefore concentrated. The bezel is chased with a composition representing cranes by the Spring of Life. The theme is Eucharistic, and the cranes are symbols of fidelity and vigilance. Doubts arise when it comes to explaining the part of the composition above a stylized chalice: if it is meant to represent a stream of water, then the composition refers to the Spring of Life guarded by the ever vigilant cranes; but if it is a heptagonal star (the symbol of Christ), then the composition ought to be interpreted in the spirit of contemporary heraldry. Similar compositions, though more stylized, are found in the Church of St. Dimitrije at Peć (1316–1324).

The ring is dated to the early 15th century on the basis of the decorative motifs on the shoulders, which are similar to motifs found on early 15th century Italian fabrics.

Historical Museum of Serbia, Belgrade
Literature: B. Radojković, (1969) pp. 120, 127–129.

8 Ring
15th century
Cast silver; chased, niello
Width: 23 mm   Bezel: 20 x 12 mm
Find from Kosovo.

The hoop has a semicircular form, profiled, and decorated with niello. The narrowest part of the hoop is chased with a sinuous vine branchlet; the sides bear linear ornament. Beneath the shoulders, the ring has a shield-shaped wider part chased with dragons. Confronted matted snakes are chased on the ring's shoulders. The bezel has a flat octagonal form with two longer sides. It is deeply engraved with a heraldic representation of a long-necked dragon's head in the form of a crest. Along the two sides are engraved five and six flowerets, respectively.

The fine execution and the massiveness of the ring prove that it was made for a nobleman (unidentified).

Although it looks like a signet ring, its real purpose is insignia. In the 15th century, Serbian noblemen often became members of the Central European knighthoods. The owner of this ring may have been a member of the chivalric Order of the Dragon.

Inv. No. 4398, Museum of Applied Art, Belgrade
Literature: B. Radojković, (1969) pp. 200–202.

9 Archer's Ring
Mid 15th century
Cast silver; chased
Height: 42 mm   Width: 30 mm
Chance find from Kosovo.

A band, semicircular in section, the bezel elongated to form a rounded triangle. The outer part embossed with four medallions, chased linear ornament, and two elongated triangles.

This ring belong to the group of luxurious rings used in sporting archery. It was made before the final arrival of the Turks in Serbia.

Inv. No. 4339, Museum of Applied Art, Belgrade
Literature: B. Radojković, (1969) p. 207.

10 Archer's Ring
Late 15th century
Cast silver; chased
Height: 40 mm   Width: 26 mm
Found in the Ramu Fortress near Golubac, Serbia.

The bezel is elongated so as to form a rounded triangle. The ring is superficially chased with a flower, two triangles with trefoils, and interlacing Gothic floral motifs with trefoil ivy.
 Rings of this type were used in sporting archery, while in battle bronze rings were used.
 The particular combination of its decorative elements, in addition to the fine and subtle execution, make one believe that it is the work of a local craftsman.

Inv. No. 4438, Museum of Applied Art, Belgrade
Literature: B. Radojković, (1969) pp. 207–208.

11 Earring
Late 12th, early 13th century
Silver; granulation, filigree
Height: 45 mm   Width: 40 mm
Find from Kosovo.

The upper part of the circle of this earring is twisted together with a thinner woven filigree wire. The lower part bears three strawberry-shaped ornaments with a circle in between, intertwined with twisted wire.
 The side strawberries are formed of two corollas, each with five cross-shaped flowerets made up of granules. The central strawberry is in the form of a cylinder made up of six lines of granules with the outermost bearing cross-shaped flowerets. The simple and precise execution of this earring reveals the high level of craftsmanship reached at that time by Serbian silversmiths.

Inv. No. 10019, Museum of Applied Art, Belgrade.

12 Earring
Early 13th century
Cast gold; filigree, granulation
Height: 55 mm
Chance find from the village of Vitovnica, Serbia.

Three strawberry-shaped ornaments cluster on the lower part of this elliptical ring, circular in section. Made up of a twisted filigree wire, they have prismatic form with round surfaces, imitating open-work. Earrings of the strawberry type existed in many variants in the Balkans. Archaeologists often come across them in the area between the Adriatic and Rila, Bulgaria.

Inv. No. 2799, National Museum, Belgrade
Literature: B. Radojković, *Serbian Goldsmiths' work of the 16th and 17th Centuries,* (Novi Sad 1966) p. 43; *ibid.* (1969) p. 97.

10

13 Earring
13th century
Cast silver; filigree, granulation
Height: 76 mm   Width: 40 mm
Archaeological find from the village of Neresnica near Zaječar, Serbia.

A circle, its upper half without decoration, the lower part bearing six symmetrically set rings with radial granules (one ring is missing). The central ornament has a conical form with the top turned towards the centre of the circle. From its base downwards overlap tiny hemispheres with flowerets made up of granules on top of them. The cone is decorated with a corolla of granules near its upmost part and a band of wound-up twisted wire beneath. Three lines of filigree wires are wound up around the base. The space between the bands is divided into larger isosceles triangles with smaller granules set in them.
  Pendent earrings of this shape originated with Byzantine jewellery, but the earliest model for this variant is the early Slavic earring with ornament in the form of an oak apple.

Inv. No. 5574, National Museum, Belgrade
Literature: D. Milošević, *Art in Mediaeval Serbia from the 12th to the 17th century,* (Belgrade 1980) Cat. No. 187.

14 Earrings (a pair of)
13th century
Cast silver; pseudo filigree, filigree, granulation
Width: 55 mm
Find from the surroundings of Skoplje, Macedonia.

The upper part of the ring has no decoration. On the lower part, on either side of an ovoid strawberry, the ring bears two pressed rosettes made up of granules. Between them and the strawberry, the ring is cast in the form of a rope.
  The strawberry is large; it begins with rosettes composed of granules. Vertically over the strawberry there extends a thicker twisted wire ornamented on either side with a line of smaller and bigger granules.
  The manufacture of jewels of this kind illustrates the economic burgeoning of the mediaeval Serbian state and the connections between Serbian and Byzantine jewellery.

Inv. No. 155, Museum of Applied Art, Belgrade
Literature: B. Radojković, *Art-Work in Metal,* II, (Belgrade 1956) Cat. No. 123.

12

14

15 Earring
13th–14th century
Cast silver; fretwork, granulation, filigree
Width: 46 mm
Find from Prilep, Macedonia.

The upper part of the ring is twisted together with another thin filigree wire. Three rings are set in its lower part, two of them in the form of hollow balls with pierced circles. The central strawberry, the biggest, is divided into two parts by a vertical strip of twisted wires with a series of larger granules arranged along the middle.

To the left and right of the strip, rising radially, there are four cones, each ending with four granules. The bases of the cones are hemmed with twisted wires, and between them as well as in the joins of the ring are set tiny triangles made up of granules.

The earliest model for this type of earring originated in Byzantium, but domestic craftsmen added certain details to it. Earrings of this type were widely diffused in the Balkans.

Inv. No. 156, Museum of Applied Art, Belgrade
Literature: B. Radojković, (1969) p. 97.

18

16 Earrings (a pair of)
Mid 14th century
Cast silver; filigree, silver-gilt, semiprecious stones
Height: 70 mm   Width 75 mm
Excavated at Marva Varoš near Prilep, Macedonia.

Of the radial type. The middle part of each contains a highly stylized bird with spread wings, executed in the fretwork and filigree techniques. A gem is set in the chest of each bird. From this part three truncated cones, two of which are narrower and one wider, spread radially and alternating. The narrower cones end with rosettes in filigree, and the larger ones with filigree-fringed bigger gems. Each wider conical ornament bears on one side shield-shaped filigree ornament. There is only one curved earring clasp on the pair (the other is lost).

Earrings of this type have been unearthed at a large number of sites, which means that they were widespread in the 14th century.

In the 14th-century, earrings in general, including this type, were made in ever larger and more luxurious forms, which is a reflexion of the favourable socio-economic conditions in the stable state which lasted until the invasion of the Turks. This type of earrings is also found in the 14th century frescoes of Bela Crkva, in the portrait of the daughter of Brahan, the Head of a tribal state, and also in the 14th century portrait of a squire's wife in the Church of Donja Kamenica.

Inv. No. 308, National Museum, Belgrade
Literature: M. Ćorović – Ljubinković, A find from Markova Varoš near Prilep, *Museums*, II, (Belgrade 1949) pp. 102–113; B. Radojković, (1956) Cat. No. 188; ibid., (1966) p. 43; ibid., (1969) p. 25; ibid., 'Mediaeval Metal Work' in *The History of Applied Art in Serbia,* Vol. I, (Belgrade 1977) p. 91.

17 Earring
Second half of the 14th century
Silver; filigree, granulation, silver-gilt
Height: 50 mm   Width: 65 mm   Diameter: 15 mm
Chance find from the surroundings of Vršac, Vojvodina.

The radial type of earring. Truncated cones fan out from the central lunular part with a finial of corollas of twisted wires. The ends of the thinner cones are ornamented with rosettes in filigree, and the three thicker ones with white stones in settings. A series of granules flows down the middle of the thicker cones. The small semicircular fastening loop is made up of a twisted wire.

Typologically, it is very much like the pair of earrings from Markova Varoš, fitting in with the large family of Byzantine style earrings whose origin should be sought in the Orient. But the specific features given to this type by domestic craftsmen are probably the reason why the people of Dubrovnik called these earrings, 'ad modum slavicum'.

Ethnographic Museum, the Crnilović Collection, Belgrade
Literature: B. Radojković, (1966) fig. 46; D. Milošević, *Mediaeval Art in Serbia,* (Belgrade 1969) Cat. No. 216; ibid., (1980) Cat. No. 198.

18 Earring
First half of 15th century
Gold; filigree, pearls, emerald, ruby
Height: 26 mm   Width: 12 x 10 mm
Archaeological find from the Fortress of Smederevo, Serbia, 1968.

The tiny tablet with a fastening loop on the top of this earring is divided by a twisted wire into six horizontal fields. Set in the middle of the square fields are large pearls, perforated with a gold wire, and an emerald and ruby. Sidewise, in the corners of the fields, are set pairs of pearls.

With its intact pearls this is a unique survival. It supports statements in mediaeval records about highly valuable Serbian earrings.

National Museum, Smederevo
Literature: B. Radojković, (1969) p. 212; ibid., 'Les métiers d'art dans la Serbie moravienne,' *Zbornik Filozofskog fakulteta (simpozijum: Moravska škola i njeno doba - [The Moravska School and its Era]),* (Belgrade 1972) p. 205; ibid., 'Mediaeval Metalwork', (1977) p. 92.

19 Earring
15th century
Cast silver; wrought, filigree
Height: 37 mm
Find from Kosovo, Serbia.

A filigree wire wound sideways up one part of the semicircular loop. The wire ends with two small rosettes separated from each other by a simple flower with ten petals.

Inv. No. 10021, Museum of Applied Art, Belgrade.

20 Earrings (a pair of)
Mid 15th century
Silver; filigree
Height: 80 mm
Find from an excavated storeroom at Peć, Kosovo, Serbia.

A semicircular ring with two ornamented strawberries executed in fretwork; two rosettes in filigree beneath. The central ornament has a radial form divided into eight pear-shaped ornaments with rosettes, tiny tubes and trembling lunules in the base. The pears are decorated with granules and tubes, and all this forms fishbone ornament. Another strawberry is set, as a finial, on top of the central ornament.

This type of earring represents an intervening variant between the earrings with three strawberries and those with pear-shaped pendants.

Inv. No. 6946, Museum of Applied Art, Belgrade
Literature: B. Radojković, (1969) Cat. No. 150.

20

21 Earring
End of 15th century
Cast alloy with silver
Height: 75 mm Width: 33 mm
Find from Kosovo.

The rectangular small tablet ornamented with rosettes at the angles and with three smaller ones on each side. One side decorated with cast rosettes and dotted ornament. A semicircular fastening loop in the upper part, and a perforated tassel in the lower.

This earring belongs to the time when craftsmen still cherished a definite type, form, and ornament; but, because of the then unfavourable political situation, the quality of the material was poorer.

Inv. No. 8194, Museum of Applied Art, Belgrade
Literature: B. Radojković, (1969) p. 248.

21

22 Bracelet
Mid 14th century
Silver; filigree, granulation, silver-gilt
Height: 33 mm Width: 60 mm
Unearthed at Markova Varoš near Prilep, Macedonia.

The large hinged bracelet is made of thin sheet silver and decorated with filigree and granular ornament, and is two-fold and symmetrical.

This type of bracelet is a borrowing from Byzantium where it was in use in various forms from the 5th century. Despot Oliver's bracelets in his fresco portrait at the Monastery of Lesnovo are similar to this piece.

Inv. No. 309, National Museum, Belgrade
Literature: B. Radojković, (1969) pp. 147–148.

23 Bracelet
Mid 14th century
Silver; filigree, granulation, silver-gilt
Height: 30 mm Width: 66 mm
Find from Markova Varoš near Prilep, Macedonia. (Five bracelets of the same type were unearthed)

A tablet-shaped bracelet of the closed type, on a hinge, made of thin sheet-silver. Two bands framed with twisted wires filled up with circlets, flow along the rims of the bracelet with symmetrical ornament in between. Along the two bands are arranged a series of arcades touching one another with their tops; larger granules are set in their points of contact. Each arcade contains a small triangle formed of tiny granules; all the triangles are pointed towards the tops of the arcades. Granules are also set in the middle of the fields between the arcades. Bracelets of this type (and Cat. No. 12) originated with Byzantine royal apparel; afterwards, they were adopted by noblemen and then by townsmen. Such bracelets were an integral part of costumes, forming the cuffs of garments.

Inv. No. 312, National Museum, Belgrade
Literature: B. Radojković, (1969) pp. 148–150.

24 Garland

Circa mid 14th century
Silver; filigree, silver-gilt, semiprecious stones
Length: 214 mm   Width: 20 mm
Unearthed at Markova Varoš near Prilep, Macedonia.

Composed of eight interconnected small tablets. Each tablet bears one semiprecious stone in a setting; the free surfaces decorated either with filigree leaflets or with conjoined rosettes. This type of head decoration originated directly with Byzantine royal jewellery and, more precisely, with the lily-*Sthemategirion*. The wreath was worn over the hair or scarf and it looked like real floral decoration on the head of a woman.

Inv. No. 316, National Museum, Belgrade
Literature: M. Ljubinković, (1949) pp. 103–113; B. Radojković, (1969) pp. 142–3; ibid., 'Medieval Metalwork', (1977) p. 92.

25 Wreath

Second half of 14th century
Silver; embossed and gilt
Height: 40 mm   Width of tablet: 35 mm
Unearthed in the Necropolis of Hajdučka Vodenica (Djerdap – the Iron Gate).

Composed of small rectangular tablets framed by dotted ornament. A wreath of branchy acanthus twigs flows around the rim with a larger oak leaf in the middle. The floral motifs on this forehead ornament almost certainly originate with the similarly stylized motifs found on the work of goldsmiths of the 14th century Dalmatian towns.

Archaeological Institute of SANU, Belgrade
Literature: B. Radojković. (1969) p. 219; D. Milošević, (1969) Cat. No. 287.

26 Forehead Ornament

End of 14th century
Stamped silver; silver-gilt
Height: 60 mm   Width of tablet: 43 mm
Find from an excavated storeroom in Požarevac, Serbia.

Composed of ten small rectangular tablets with a semicircular addition on the top. The lower part bears a griffon in profile. Beneath the griffon, in an arcade, a heraldic charge (deltoid, with bends and starlets, and a stylized fleur-de-lis). Ornament of straight lines frames the tablets. Between them are set smaller square plates.

The shape of these small tablets corresponds to that of the jewels in the fresco-portrait of the feudal lady Kalina, in the monastery of Stari Grad at Prespa, and the griffon to those on the garment worn by the Grand Duke Lazar.

Inv. No. 318, Historical Museum of Serbia, Belgrade
Literature: B. Radojković, (1969) p. 219; D. Milošević, Cat. No. 288.

26

24

27 Forehead Ornament
Late 14th–early 15th century
Stamped silver; silver-gilt
Height: 54 mm   Width of tablet: 43 mm
Archaeological find from an excavated storeroom in the surroundings of Požarevac, Serbia.

Composed of large rectangular tablets with the upper end in the form of a Saracenic arch, and smaller square tablets set between the larger ones. In the middle of the larger tablets stands the Tree of Life with a twisted trunk; set beside it are two addorsed birds with only their heads turned towards the trunk. The tablets are edged with straight lines. The model for these tablets should be sought in Italian decorative art of the 14th and early 15th century.

Inv. No. 2458, Historical Museum of Serbia, Belgrade
Literature: B. Radojković, (1969) p. 219; D. Milošević, (1969) Cat. No. 289.

27

28 Forehead Ornament
Mid 15th century
Stamped silver
Height: 48 mm   Width of tablet: 40 mm
Find from around Peć, Kosovo.

Rectangular tablets with repeating motifs: Gothic trefoils, fleur-de-lis, spear-shaped ornament and rosettes, framed by dotted ornament.

Inv. No. 6947, Museum of Applied Art, Belgrade
Literature: B. Radojković, (1969) p. 219.

28

29 Aigrette
15th century
Wrought gold, set with a stone
Height: 85 mm
Find from Serbia (site unknown).

A long flat pin with a head in the form of a lotus flower and a red stone set in it. The petals of the flower embossed with chick-pea leaflets. On the right side of the flower extend two longer plumes with leaf-shaped trembling ornament which hangs on the loops.
    This ornament was worn on womens' caps.

Inv. No. 3369, Museum of Applied Art, Belgrade
Literature: B. Radojković, (1969) Cat. No. 186.

29

30 **Necklace**
15th century
Silver; filigree, granulation
Width: 135 mm
Find from the surroundings of Peć, Kosovo.

Of the open type made up of a twisted twofold wire around
which another thinner twisted fliligree wire is wound. Six
perforated spheres composed of filigree and larger granules are
fixed to the lower part of this circular base. Woven filigree belts
are set in between the spheres. One sphere is of later date.

Inv. No. 3569, Museum of Applied Art, Belgrade
Literature: B. Radojković, (1969) Cat. No. 189.

30

31 Belt Buckle
Mid 13th century
Cast silver
Length: 77 mm Width: 25 mm
Find from around Priština, Kosovo.

The buckle is in the form of a double fleur-de-lis with a rosette in the middle and it is clasped by pulling one part through the other. The whole buckle is covered with floral ornament, and its ends are decorated with spear-shaped trefoils.
 Similarly stylized lilies are found in the frescoes at the Chapel of Studenica (c. 1234), and more precisely, in the decoration on Queen Anna's dress in her fresco-portrait.

Inv. No. 4580, Museum of Applied Art, Belgrade
Literature: B. Radojković, (1969) p. 153.

31

32 Bowl
12th–13th century
Silver; embossed, chased
Height: 75mm Width of the mouth: 70 mm
Chance find from around Arilje.

The bowl is deep, bellied, with an everted rim, narrowing towards the mouth and with a border of stylized trefoils. In the round medallions are portraits of the Evangelists, and between them, rhombuses and floral motifs. The portraits are individualized, but on the verge of typification. The figures are dignified and calm but not stiff. The cup shares in the style of the Byzantine cultural circle originating in Syria.

Inv. No. 5559, National Museum, Belgrade
Literature: B. Radojković, (1977) p. 87.

33 Bowl
13th century
Wrought silver; embossed, silver-gilt
Width: 160 mm
Chance find from around Arilje.

The bowl is shallow. The medallion on the bottom shows an eagle preying on fish. The eagle, with is head turned towards its spread left wing surmounted by a cross, holds a big fish in its claws; to the left and right of it are two curved fish following the circular line of the medallion. The medallion is composed in the Byzantine manner, yet its true source should be sought in Syrian art where such symbols of the Eucharist frequently appear.

Inv. No. 5560, National Museum, Belgrade
Literature: D. Milošević, (1980) Cat. No. 142.

34 The Sevast Čuzmen Plate
14th century
Silver; punched, chased
Height: 35 mm Width: 280 mm
Find from Serbia (site unknown).

A circular shallow dish with no decoration, reminiscent of plain late antique dishes. A circular inscription on the bottom reads: 'Sevast Čuzmen.'
 The beautifully inscribed name in Cyrillic indicates that it might have been made at the court of this feudal lord, as was customary at that time, or sent as a present from the suzerain to its later owner.

Inv. No. 1527, National Museum, Belgrade
Literature: St. Stojanović, *The Sevast Čuzmen Plate,* (Belgrade 1927); B. Radojković, (1956) Cat. No. 165; ibid., (1966) p. 27.

35 Bowl
14th century
Silver; niello, silver-gilt
Height: 37 mm   Width: 115 mm
Find from Serbia (site unknown).

Of average, shallow form, the brim lobed. In the centre of the bottom is set a round medallion with an eight-petalled flower and wavy linear ornament around it. A handle, triangular in section, on one side. The outer surface decorated with a stylized stem. A 'button' set on top of the handle.

Inv. No. 2016, Museum of the City of Belgrade
Literature: Dr. M. Birtašević-Hadži-Pešić, *A Visit to Mediaeval Belgrade (Catalogue),* (Belgrade 1978) p. 19.

35

36 Bowl
End of 14th century
Wrought silver
Height: 30 mm   Width: 135mm
Find from Serbia (site unknown).

Shallow, in the form of a skull-cap. Inside, within a circle a design in low relief of a six-petalled flower with pointed petals and trefoils between them. A wide circular band around it and another band with small arches set around the wide band. The sides of the bowl are covered with two wavy lines running upwards and downwards and forming overlapping arches; instead of capitals, the arch-ends bear sculptural trefoils turned upwards and downwards.

The linear and plant ornament on this bowl originates directly with mediaeval Serbian paintings, and its evolution can be traced from the monastery of Nerezi (1168) down to the monastery of Psača (1358).

Inv. No. 3107, Museum of Applied Art, Belgrade.

37 Bowl
Late 14th or early 15th century
Silver; wrought, chased, and gilt
Height: 42 mm   Width: 142 mm
Chance find from around Peć, Kosovo, Serbia.

In the form of a skull-cap; the centre at the bottom encircled by rope ornament, framing a now lost medallion. Three flowers alternating with three buds break out from the 'rope'. The flowers are encircled with a large band, a late Gothic hexafoil with its points between the petals.

Down the sides of the bowl flow eight garland arches pierced by leaves with stems resting on the Gothic hexafoil. Late Gothic elements as well as Oriental influences are evident in this piece.

The bowl may well have been made near where it was unearthed. The inscription reads, 'This bowl belongs to Vukašin; God help him who drinks from it.'

Inv. No. 11176, Museum of Applied Art, Belgrade.

37

38 Bowl
Late 14th, early 15th century
Wought silver; silver-gilt
Height: 40 mm   Width: 167 mm
Chance find from Serbia (site unknown).

With a convex bottom in the form of a Gothic hexafoil flower framing a central round medallion bearing a heraldic sign in low relief.

Six reversed arches are punched on the sides of the bowl and the rim of the bowl is wavy and protruding. The Gothic flower on the base is characteristic of the silver bowls manufactured in European silversmiths' workshops, in general, and in the Serbian ones in particular, at the end of the 14th and early 15th century. One comes across them everywhere from Sweden to Germany, France and Hungary, right down to the Balkans. The origin of the Gothic hexafoil or octofoil flower is found in quadrafoil medallions made up of precious or semiprecious stones worn as part of jewellery in Byzantium. In Serbia, the central medallion usually bears a heraldic sign or a bird, but after the 17th century also the figure of Christ *Pantocrator.*

Inv. No. 2689, Museum of Applied Art, Belgrade
Literature: B. Radojković, 'The Silver Cups of Serbian Origin from the Necropolis of Bela Reka; *Zbornik of the Museum of Applied Art,* XVI–XVII, (Belgrade 1972–73) pp. 23–34.

38

41

39 Bowl
Circa 1490
Silver; embossed, silver-gilt, niello
Height: 102 mm   Width: 186 mm
Find from a tomb in the Baptistery at Stobi, Macedonia.

Elliptical with a wavy rim composed of twelve fields with no
decoration. In the bottom, an arched rectangular field bears a
round plaque with a male portrait in profile and an oak leaf on
each side. To the left and right of it are set two round medallions
embossed in low relief with a walking lion and a monster. All this
is framed with ivy stems and leaves. The decorative motifs found
in this piece – the oak leaf, ivy stems, and flowerets composed of
circles – are characteristic of the whole Mediterranean area, and
particularly of Italian goldsmiths' work. From a comparison of
this bowl with the work of craftsmen of Kotor, one concludes that
it must have been manufactured either by some Kotor master
who lived in the interior of the country or some goldsmith under
the strong influence of the goldsmiths of Kotor.

The half figure of a knight in profile with his hair thrown back,
is executed completely in the manner of the Kotor craftsmen.

Inv. No. 343, National Museum, Belgrade
Literature: B. Radojković, 'Some Characteristics of Kotor's Gold-
smith's work and its Influence on the Interior,' *The Antiques of
Montenegro,* III–IV, (Cetinje 1965–6) pp. 65–67.

40 Bowl
End of 15th century
Silver; chased
Height: 28 mm   Width: 113 mm
Find from Serbia (site unknown)

The bottom of this round and shallow bowl is chased with a
circular medallion, with inside, a walking bird with half-spread
wings and head turned backwards. An inscription is chased in
the narrow band around the bird, along the edges of the medallion. Four branchlets break out of the band towards the bird.
Over the inner sides of the bowl flows a continuous strip of stems
with leaves and large flowers.

The ornament is executed in a rather naïve manner, but the
drawing of the bird is the work of a good master.

Bowls of this kind were mass-produced and never directly
ordered from the craftsman. This particular bowl was manufactured in an unknown workshop of Prizren.

Inv. No. 641, Museum of Applied Art, Belgrade
Literature: B. Radojković, (1972–73) pp. 23–34.

41 Reliquary (fragmentary)
12th–13th century
Silver; embossed; niello remnants
Height: 44 mm   Width: 22mm
Archaeological find from Markova Varoš near Prilip, Macedonia.

Only this one small wrought tablet, as part of a reliquary found in
fragments, has survived to our day. The standing figures of the
Warrior Saints (St. George, St. Demetrius, and one unidentified
saint) are represented with their clothing and arms elongated
like the ascetic figures in the paintings by the 13th century Monk
of Cappadocia. The sides of the tablet are decorated with intertwined wavy ornament and floral motifs.

Inv. No. 317, National Museum, Belgrade
Literature: M. Ćorović-Ljubinković, 'A find from Markova Varoš
near Prilep,' *Museums* II, Belgrade, 1949; B. Radojković, (1956)
Cat. No. 189; D. Milošević, (1969) Cat. No. 26; B. Radojković, *Les
objets sculptés d'art mineur en Serbie ancienne,* (Belgrade, 1977), p. 20.

43

42 Icon
13th century
Cast bronze; gilt
Height: 52 mm   Width: 42 mm   Diameter: 5 mm
Found in a wall of the Church of SS. Apostles at the Patriarchate of Peć, Kosovo, in 1933–34; kept in the National Museum, Belgrade since 1952.

A half-figure of Our Lady *Hodegetria* with Jesus on her left arm is represented in low relief. Her robe is richly draped.

This small icon reflects many stylistically different elements: precedence is given to the pictorial expression, while the proportions are neglected. The head is large, the shoulders very narrow, the neck extremely short, though both Gothic and Byzantine art paid great attention to the depiction of the neck, as well as to the form of hands and the drawing of fingers. As all this has been neglected in this small icon, it suggests that it is of provincial origin.

Inv. No. 2261, National Museum, Belgrade
Literature: D. Milošević, 'The Bronze Icon of the Virgin Mary with Jesus,' *Zbornik of the National Museum*, XXIII, (Belgrade, 1979) pp. 373–389; ibid., (1980) Cat. No. 92.

43 Hand Censer
14th century
Cast bronze; pierced
Height: 115 mm   Length: 300 mm   Width: 125 mm
Unearthed in Kosovo (Janjevo), Serbia.

Of horizontal type with the handle in the same plane; elliptical and composed of two parts: one for incense (and embers) and the other decorative, with a handle. The incense container is hemispherical, the lid is dome-shaped with perforations in the form of circles and keyholes; a cross finial is fixed on top of it.

The other part represents the Tree of Life pecked by two pairs of confronted birds. Censers of this type were introduced by monks from Mt. Athos to Serbia in the Middle Ages.

Inv. No. 161, Museum of Applied Art, Belgrade
Literature: B. Radojković, (1956) Cat. No. 171; D. Milošević, 'The Bronze Censer in the National Museum,' *Zbornik of the National Museum,* VIII, (Belgrade, 1964), p. 284.

44 Hanging Censer
14th century
Cast bronze; open work
Height: 200 mm   Width: 86 mm
Find from Serbia (site unknown).

The incense container in the form of a hemisphere divided into segments. The lid in the form of an octagonal cupola with a peak on top, and with circular, triangular, rectangular and elliptical perforations.

This censer is an example of mature Gothic. Censers of this type originated in the southern part of Germany and a large number of this type are found in Serbia, which reflects both mediaeval Serbian cultural-economic connections with Europe, and the possibility that these and similar objects were manufactured in Serbia itself.

Inv. No. 879, Museum of Applied Art, Belgrade
Literature: B. Radojković, 'Imports of mediaeval copper and bronze objects from Europe to the territories of Serbia and Belgrade,' *The Annual Almanac of the Museum of the City of Belgrade,* XXV, Cat. No. 978, pp. 177–184.

44

45 Censer
End of 14th century
Cast bronze; open work
Height: 205 mm
From the monastery of Ljubostinja.

Standing on a profiled hexagonal foot, the censer resembles an irregular prism with the lid in the form of a Gothic tower with a Greek cross finial. The tower is executed in open-work with ornament of small stylized crosses and six-petalled flowers.

Three small chains for carrying the censer are fixed to the edges of its body, and their upper ends are joined with a loop.

This censer clearly reflects the Gothic influence exerted on Serbian goldsmiths' work in the 14th century from Italy via the Adriatic coast, and from Central Europe down the Danube.

Inv. No. 2256, National Museum, Belgrade
Literature: M. Valtrović, 'Travel Notes', *Starinar,* V, (Belgrade 1888), p. 4; D. Milošević, (1980) Cat. No. 105.

46 Censer
End of 15th century
Cast silver; embossed; filigree and granulation
Height: 240 mm   Height with chains: 750 mm
The Treasury of the monastery of Dečani, Kosovo.

On a hexagonal foot which is profiled and decorated with filigree and granules stands the round body of this richly ornamented censer. From its rim soar four smaller Gothic towers with sphere finials; its centre bears a taller tower with a Greek cross, three arms of which end in trefoils. Gothic windows, each with twelve openings, are built in the towers and cast griffons on the pilasters.

The censer is carried by five chains with small round bells, joining at the upper end in a large profiled handle. The composition of Gothic decorative motifs and towers is characteristic: the leaflets are free but realistic; the towers are thicker and the windows reminiscent of Gothic biforms.

Stylistically, this type of censer can be associated with Adriatic coastal craftsmanship, and particularly with the goldsmiths' workshops of Dubrovnik.

Treasury of the monastery of Dečani
Literature: B. Radojković, (1956) Cat. No. 280; ibid., (1966) pp. 125–6; ibid., 'Mediaeval Metalwork' (1977) p. 86.

45

46

47 Pectoral Pendant (Icon)
14th century
Carved rhinoceros horn
Width: 150 mm
From the Treasury of the monastery of Dečani, Kosovo.

Executed in high relief. The Virgin with Jesus as the incarnation of the Word is in the centre, with half-figures of saints above the Virgin's head; the Deisis and Holy Fathers, Deacons and Apostles are arrayed in the arcades along the rim. The whole scene is composed as a version of the Divine Liturgy. Comparison with the pectoral pendant in the monastery of Xeropotham (Mt. Athos), the so-called Pulcheria pendant made of steatite, has shown that the two pectoral pendants are very close to each other, both stylistically and iconographically. Another comparison, this time with the 'Hilandar' pectoral pendant of horn, leads one to the conclusion, however, that the pectoral pendant of Dečani originated at the same time as the former (14th century).

These three examples are the most valuable of a big family of 14th century stone and horn pectoral pendants. They had a precise purpose in Court and Church ceremonies: they used to be put on the altar as a plate for the bread and later, when set in silver mounts and with prayers to the Virgin Mary chased on them, they were worn on the chest by ecclesiastical dignitaries.

Treasury of the monastery of Dečani
Literature: M. Jevrić, 'La Panagie du trésor du monastère Dečani,' *Actes du XIIe Congrès international d'Études byzantines,* III, (Belgrade, 1964) pp. 151–7, fig. 1–3; B. Radojković, (1966) p. 26; and V. Han, 'Mediaeval Bone and Horn,' *The History of Applied Arts in Serbia,* Vol. I. (Belgrade, 1977) p. 185.

47

48 Chalice
End of 15th century
Silver alloy; wrought, silver-gilt
Height: 275 mm   Width of mouth: 125 mm
Width of foot: 135 mm
From the Treasury of the monastry of Banja near Priboj, Serbia.

On a hexagonal lobed foot with a profiled handle stands a waisted, deep cup. Ornament executed in open-work on the foot.

The chalice is stylistically very pure, and, in respect of craftsmanship, very well executed.

Inv. No. 31, Treasury of the monastery of Banja near Priboj
Literature: D. Milošević, (1980) Cat. No. 107; M. Sakota, *The Treasury of Banja Monastery,* (Belgrade, 1981) pp 62–66.

49 Plaque
15th century
Cast bronze; gilt
Width: 90 mm
Archaeological find from Lazarev Grad in Kruševac, Serbia.

A medallion with, on its edge, a band of stylized plant ornament executed in open-work. Inside, the medallion is a lion passant, with its tail ending in a rich palmette. A luxuriant wreath of flowers encircles the lion.

In the Moravska school the lion appears frequently as a heraldic symbol in all the arts.

Inv. No. 1447, National Museum, Kruševac
Literature: D. Milošević, (1980) Cat. No. 246.

50

50 Ring
17th century
Silver; filigree, granulation, set with an intaglio
Width: 20 mm
Find from Serbia (site unknown).

The hoop of the ring is round (semicircular in section) with broader shoulders whose triangular surfaces are decorated with applied flowerets of filigree and granules. An early Christian intaglio with the figure of a Holy Warrior is set in the elliptical bezel. A double rope and dotted ornament encircle the bezel.

Inv. No. 698, Museum of Applied Art, Belgrade.

51 Earrings
16th–17th century
Cast silver; filigree, granulation
Height: 70 mm   Width: 55 mm
Manufactured in a workshop at Prizren, Kosovo.

Of the radial type: round earrings in the form of rosettes with convex central parts, ornamented with poppyheads along the edges. Trefoil ornament set in a shield-shaped medallion on the loop for clasping the ring. A rosette with the same motif on the back.

Earrings of this kind were also decorated with enamel, and continued to be made up to the first half of the 19th century, when they took on elements of Serbian folk art.

Inv. No. 4097, Museum of Applied Art, Belgrade.

52 Earrings (with a braided silver band)
17th century
Cast silver; wrought; filigree, granulation
Height: 80 mm   Weight: 58 mm   Length of the band: 740 mm
Find from Kosovo.

The upper part bears a large loop for holding the band. The lower part is the body of the earring with an extracted semicircular segment at the top. Set in the centre is a faceted red glass paste, with five larger wrought beads around it. The whole surface is filled with filigree and tiny granules; the back surface is wrought with arrays of circlets. The connecting band is composed of intertwined silver wires.

Earring of this type were worn connected by the braided silver band which was thrown over the head. Their decoration corresponds to contemporary Turkish decoration, and they are found over a wide area of Serbia.

This is one of the few completely preserved examples of this type.

Inv. No. 7772, Museum of Applied Art, Belgrade.

51

52

53 Earrings

17th century
Cast silver; filigree, granulation and pseudo-granulation, silver-gilt
Width: 65 mm
Archaeological find from an excavated storeroom in Niš, Serbia.

Round, in the form of sculptural rosettes. The back decorated with stylized plant ornament executed in filigree.

Inv. No. 8189, Museum of Applied Art, Belgrade.

54 Bracelet

Early 16th century
Cast silver; perforated, chased, silver-gilt
Height: 28 mm   Length: 175 mm
Find from Okhrid, Macedonia.

Of the closed type; hinged, and composed of small bent tablets decorated in open-work with a Eucharistic scene showing two confronted peacocks drinking from the Spring of Life.
    The iconographical roots of this are in the Moravska school of painting, but here it can be regarded simply as a decorative feature. At this time the bracelet was enjoying a revival, for while in the middle ages it had been worn as an integral part of the clothing, under the influence of the Turks it began to be worn independently.

Inv. No. 154, Museum of Applied Art, Belgrade
Literature: B. Radojković, (1969) p. 257

55 Belt (fragment)

15th century
Cast silver; granulation, silver-gilt
Length: 85 mm
Archaeological find from Niš, Serbia.

Composed of three lines of small berries of ovoid form. The whole decorated with pyramids of small granules, ornaments of pseudo-filigree and details of linear ornament. Two small parallel tablets fringed with filigree wire and granules are set in the middle of the belt.
    The reverse is decorated with monsters in low relief.

Inv. No. 6944, Museum of Applied Art, Belgrade.
Literature: B. Radojković, (1959) Cat. No. 192.

54

55

53

56 Belt (fragment)
16th century
Cast silver; open work, chased
Length: 150 mm
Find from the village of Babune near Priština, Kosovo.

Composed of three tablets, the two smaller ones rectangular and identical. The bigger tablet is also in the form of a rectangle, but with an oval arch protruding from one side of it; four clasps are fixed to the opposite side. This tablet is ornamented in open-work with a stylized Tree of Life, chick-pea stems and spear-shaped trefoils. A band of naïve stylized lilies flows along the edge. The two smaller tablets are chased with chick-pea stems, four-petalled flowers and, in the centre, crossed tulips.
     The decoration on this belt clearly reflects the dominant characteristics of 16th century Serbian goldsmiths' work: late Gothic motifs, mediaeval ornamentation, and Turkish decoration.

Inv. No. 167, Museum of Applied Art, Belgrade
Literature: B. Radojković, (1969) Cat. No. 121.

57 Belt Buckle
16th century
Cast silver
Length: 170mm   Width: 53 mm
Find from Kosovo, Serbia (site unknown).

Composed of three parts: two rectangular tablets with protruding arched ends and one S-shaped thorn. The tablets are fringed with chick-pea stems; the centre of each tablet is ornamented with a Turkish shield-shaped medallion with arabesques. The thorn is decorated with notches.
     All the decoration on this buckle is in the spirit of 16th century Islamic ornamentation.

Inv. No. 4589, Museum of Applied Art, Belgrade
Literature: B. Radojković, (1969) p. 254.

58 Belt
16th–17th century
Cast silver; open work, silver-gilt
Height: 55 mm   Length: 950 mm
Find from an unknown locality in Serbia.

The clasps are rectangular, with arched ends decorated with two highly stylized Trees of Life in open-work. The belt is composed of a textile band with small tablets slipped over it. The faces of the tablets are S-shaped with snakes' heads at the ends. An eight-petalled flower is in the centre of each tablet. The tablets are decorated with plant ornament.
     Turkish influence can clearly be seen in the decoration.

Inv. No. 10035, Museum of Applied Art, Belgrade
Literature: B. Radojković, (1969) Cat. No. 213.

58

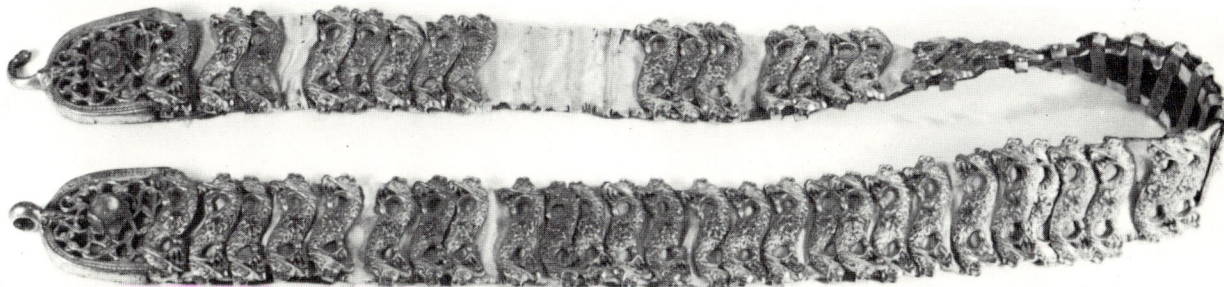

59 Belt

17th century
Cast silver; wrought, chased
Length: 450 mm   Width: 145 mm
Bought in Herzegovina.

Five square tablets cast with an identical scene: St. Demetrius slaughtering the infidel Czar Kalayan. Behind him is a tree with a bird, and in front of him, stylized architecture. Each tablet is framed by a band of stylized sinuous stems with trefoils. The central raised tablet ends with an arch of Saracenic type. This space bears a cross with stylized lilies between the arms.

The naïvely treated composition with St. Demetrius and the exceptionally subtly executed plant decoration reflect the tendency for Turkish art gradually to oust the human figure from Serbian goldsmiths' work in favour of ornament.

Inv. No. 10026, Museum of Applied Art, Belgrade
Literature: B. Radojković, (1956) Cat. No. 113.

60 Bowl

1520–30s
Silver; niello (or enamel?)
Height: 75 mm   Width: 66 mm
Found in Temska near Pirot, Serbia.

Elliptical, and divided into eighteen segments. A rectangular medallion with curved corners is set in the base, and within a rope border is a panther with its tail erect in the shape of a palmette.

Comparison with German lobed cups suggest that this piece dates from the early 16th century, and is in true late Gothic style.

Ethnographic Museum, Belgrade
Literature: V. Han, 'Une coupe d'argent de la Serbie medievale,' *Actes du XIIe Congrès international d'Etudes byzantine,* (Belgrade, 1964) III; B. Radojković, (1966) p. 35.

59

60

1a

1b

61 **Incense Boat**

1523

Silver; engraved, embossed, enamelled

Length: 295 mm   Width: 54 mm   Height: 100 mm

Manufactured in Smederevo for the monastery of Ravanica.

A boat-shaped vessel with everted upper ends representing the heads of Chimeras. On the bottom an elliptical medallion engraved with a symbolical Eucharistic scene with a confronted dog and lion and the Spring of Life. A bird is engraved on top of the lion's head. The medallion was once decorated with blue and green champlevé enamel, of which traces remain. The inner sides of the boat are engraved with elephants, lions and birds encircled by a stylized vine. Two triangular tablets at the ends bear allegorical representations.

This piece was made in 1523 for Dionisije (Dionysius), the Prior of Ravanica Monastery, as recorded by the inscription around the outer edge.

The work clearly reflects Turco-Persian influences. Being made in the first quarter of the 16th century, it demonstrates the speed with which Persian art influenced Turkish goldsmiths' work and through it, also the Serbian craftsmanship of the day.

The composition on the bottom originates in very ancient Persian art, but by the 16th century it had a purely decorative function without any symbolical or allegorical significance. This incense boat is the work of an exceptionally skilled master who probably belonged to the important goldsmithing centre in Smederevo, the onetime seat of Serbian Despots.

Museum of the Serbian Orthodox Church, Belgrade

Literature: B. Radojković, (1966) pp. 104–105; ibid., (1965) pp. 126–7, 129.

62 Bowl

First half of 16th century
Silver; chased, silver-gilt
Height: 35 mm   Width: 140 mm
Provenance unknown.

In the form of a skull-cap with a convex centre bearing an applied
round medallion embossed with a decorative figurine in the
middle. The medallion is chased with leaves and flowers and a
band of vines and leaflets flows around it. From the band out-
wards flows stylized ornament. A composition depicting hunting
is in the frieze on the side of the cup. A Renaissance vine with
flowers and leaves creates open medallions with alternating
pairs of animals: dog and deer, hare and dog, wild boar and lion,
lion killing doe, hare and fox. One medallion is chased with a
kneeling hunter drawing his bow. The base of the bowl is chased
with an inscription by its former owner, the priest Jovančević,
dating from 1830. On the underside there is a typical silver
assaying scratch.

   The cup was manufactured in one of the Dubrovnik workshops; it is a typical example of the combined influences from
Italy and Turkey.

Inv. No. 2907, Museum of Applied Art, Belgrade
Literature: B. Radojković, 'The Renaissance Silver Cup in the
Museum of Applied Art, Belgrade,' *Zbornik of the Museum of
Applied Art,* VI–VII, (Belgrade 1960–61) pp. 7–17.

63 Bowl

16th century
Silver; wrought, chased, silver-gilt
Height: 40 mm   Width: 130 mm
Bought in Peć, Kosovo.

A shallow bowl with everted round foot and flat bottom. In the
base is a round medallion chased in low relief with confronted
peacocks drinking from a large chalice. Above the chalice there is
a trefoil. The whole is framed by a vine with heart-shaped leaves.
Dotted ornament is chased around the edge of the medallion.
A stag couchant with gilt horns is pinned to the centre of the
medallion.

   The sides of the bowl are encompassed by two bands of wide
ribbed ornament crossed at three points by undulating medallions with floral motifs.

Inv. No. 1159, Museum of Applied Art, Belgrade
Literature: B. Radojković, (1956) Cat. No. 368.

62

63

64 Bowl

Second half of 16th century
Silver; embossed, chiselled, silver-gilt
Height: 39 mm   Width 110 mm
Find from Serbia (site unknown).

A round bowl with convex base. The medallion with floral ornament embossed with a headless animal, probably a deer. The
insides of the bowl are divided into five-arched arcades with
Saracenic arches and broad capitals supported by slender
columns with three large leaves at the base of each. Within the
arcades, executed in low relief, are a Silenus with a shepherd's
flute, an owl, a greyhound, hare, raven, modified sphinx, and a
pelican.

The bowl was manufactured in the Balkan interior; its finely
executed animal and human figures were in origin symbolical
but their function here is for the most part decorative.

Inv. No. 1570, National Museum, Belgrade
Literature: M. Tatić, (1969) Cat. No. 160; D. Milošević, (1980) Cat.
No. 149.

65 Bowl

1592–3
Silver; embossed, chiselled, silver-gilt
Height: 45 mm   Width: 190 mm
From the monastery of Dečani, Kosovo.

A medallion with floral ornamentation on the base, with, around
it, a decorative strip of leaves with wolves chasing roe deer.
Inside the rim is a wide band with animals and vines in low relief:
a lion passant, an eagle with spread wings, a roe deer, a grazing
stag, hares, a dog chasing a doe, a water bird with snake, and
three dogs.

The bowl is unmarked, but its execution suggests that it was
manufactured in a Dubrovnik workshop. The inscription engrav-
ed on the underside says that it was purchased by the Novo Brdo
Metropolitan, Victor, and donated by him to the monastery of
Dečani. At that time a big Dubrovnik colony existed at Novo
Brdo.

This bowl is one of the most beautiful art objects in metal of the
16th century to survive to this day. The cup was bought and
donated in memory of 'the old man, Petronius, and for the peace
of his soul'.

Treasury of the monastery of Dečani
Literature: B. Radojković, (1956) Cat. No. 277.

66 Bowl

17th century
Silver; wrought, chased, silver-gilt
Height: 30 mm   Width: 168 mm
Find from Serbia (site unknown).

A shallow bowl with wide sides and convex bottom, in the centre
of which there was once a medallion. Around this is a twisted
'rope' with protruding flowers and leaves. The sides bear three
lobed medallions with an eagle, a couchant greyhound, and a
moving greyhound. Between them are three more lobed medallions with floral ornament consisting of a fruit with a protruding
stylized flower. On the sides are two late Gothic twisted flowers.
Each space between the medallions is chased with two vertical
branchlets flowering at the ends and caught at the middle by a
ribbon.

The medallions on this bowl are copies of earlier medallions
from an unknown object, but the other decorative motifs are
contemporary, while the Italianate laurel branchlets date back to
Gothic times. It was manufactured by an unknown goldsmith of
Dubrovnik.

Inv. No. 6724, Museum of Applied Art, Belgrade
Literature: B. Radojković, (1972–3) pp. 23–24.

66

67 Bowl
17th century
Wrought silver; chased
Width: 130 mm
Chance find from Banjica.
Donated to the church of Ježevačka Crkva which eventually gave it to the Museum of the City of Belgrade; the latter presented it to the Museum of Applied Art in Belgrade.

Round, with a convex bottom and a circular medallion with intertwined vines and leaves in the centre. The medallion is encircled by a band of interlaced zigzag lines. The inner surface is decorated with oblique leaf-shaped ornament ending in Saracenic arches filled with leaflets and flowerets. The inner final is in the form of a dotted garland. The outer finial is a decorative band of plant ornament.

The bowl is executed in the Herzegovinian manner under the influence of Islamic ornamentation.

Inv. No. 639, Museum of Applied Art, Belgrade.

68 Bowl
Circa 1650
Wrought silver; embossed, parcel-gilt
Height: 42 mm   Width 170 mm
Find from Serbia (site unknown).

Deep and round, with a convex bottom in the centre. The round medallion encircled with an eight-petalled flower bearing deltoid designs between the petals is decorated with a half-figure of St. Nicholas blessing with his right hand and holding a book in his left. The inner surface is decorated with arcades having stylized Saracenic arches which shelter twelve standing figures of Serbian saints confronted in pairs. The columns supporting the vaults are obliquely notched and ornamented with trefoils instead of capitals.

The figures and decoration are gilt and in low relief. All the figures are executed according to a stereotype, but they nevertheless reveal the artist's effort to give individual traits to each of them.

In addition to the influence of Islamic art, this cup also reflects the influence of 14th century Serbian frescoes. It is probably the work of the Master Luka of Ćiprovac.

Inv. No. 6723, Museum of Applied Art, Belgrade
Literature: B. Radojković, (1966) pp. 148, 150–1.

67

68

69 Jug
15th–16th century
Cast lead; chased
Height: 310 mm   Width 220 mm
Unearthed in the surroundings of Gnjilane, Serbia.

Container in the form of a slightly flattened ball, set on four small feet with no ornament.

Decorated with two identical medallions with a scene in low relief symbolical of the Eucharist: a vase in the middle with a smaller one on top, and a stylized water fountain; a jet of water spurting from the smaller vase with two confronted birds drinking from it; to the left and right of the vase, two addorsed lions in profile.

The medallions are richly decorated with notches and linear ornament.

Above each medallion is set a semicircular wreath of cogs in double file.

The handles, one with a spout, are in the form of an overturned 'L' leaning symmetrically on the neck which slightly widens upwards.

Both handles are decorated with three stylized sculptural dragons' heads and luxuriant low-relief sinuous vines, leaves and flowers.

Inv. No. 784, Museum of Applied Art, Belgrade
Literature: B. Radojković, 'A Jug with a Eucharistic Scene,' *Zbornik of the Museum of Applied Art,* II, (Belgrade 1956) pp. 27–43.

70 Cross

1551

Carved cherry wood; chased silver; facetted stones
Height: 270 mm   Width: 105 mm   Depth: 25 mm
From the village of Smire, Serbia.

The long vertical arm mounted on a longer handle (round in
section) with three rings. Simple arcades on both sides of the
cross frame four scenes from the life of Jesus Christ, and two
Evangelists on each side. The scenes are executed in low relief.
The cross is mounted in chased silver set with ten semiprecious
red and blue stones on the sides.

Inconographically this cross can be traced back to Byzantium,
and stylistically to the west. It originated under the influence of
the Italo-Byzantine school of painting, particularly under that
part of it which radiated towards the Balkans from Venice. It
belongs to the group of the oldest surviving dated crosses
designed for kissing by the faithful. The inscription on the
handle refers to the Metropolitan who commissioned the cross,
and it is very likely that he did some of the actual work on it.

He was the Metropolitan Nikanor, who presented the cross to
his foundation, the church of the Ascension near the village of
Smire. Stojan Novaković found the cross at the monastery of
Rajinovac in 1875.

Inv. No. 1560, National Museum, Belgrade
Literature: R. Ljubinković, 'The Two Gračanica Icons with Portraits
of the Metropolitans Nikanor and Victor,' *Starinar* V–VI, (Belgrade
1956) pp. 130–1; B. Radojković, (1977) p. 36.

71 Cross

Mid 17th century
Cast silver; open work, silver-gilt, carved olive wood, cornelian, cut glass
Height: 350 mm   Width: 125 mm
Find from Serbia (site unknown).

The simple handle (polygonal in section) with a prism at the bottom has a ring with a spiral coil over its middle part. The mounts of the cross are executed in low relief with open work ornament with a motif of intertwined multiple vines.

Set on the sides and above are four cornelians and a red paste. The cross also bears thirty four applied flowers set with small balls of glass in the centres.

The small arcades with the Saracenic arches shelter the following scenes in high relief:

Obverse, centre: the Baptism of Christ; left: an Evangelist; right: another Evangelist; above: the Annunciation; below: the Purification of the Virgin Mary; and bottom: the Holy Church.

Reverse, centre: the Crucifixion; above: the Resurrection (the Descent into Hell variant); left and right: the Evangelists; below: the Visitation; bottom: the Bathing of Jesus Christ.

The cross was manufactured in one of the Herzegovinian workshops and it ranks among the best works from that period.

Inv. No. 7022, Museum of Applied Art, Belgrade
Literature: B. Radojković, 'Three Works of Serbian Goldsmiths from the 16th, 17th and 18th centuries.' *Zbornik of the Museum of Applied Art,* XIII, (Belgrade 1969) p. 78.

72 Cross
1650
Silver; filigree, silver-gilt, carved wood
Height: 293 mm   Width: 100mm
Donated to the monastery of Krušedol, Serbia.

A hand cross, designed for kissing by the faithful. The long handle (circular in section) begins with a prism decorated with filigree and stones. The middle part of the handle has a knop of five-fold silver wire. The mounts are made of silver and decorated with filigree or chasing and stones. The scenes on the cross are placed in arcades with Saracenic arches The scenes on the obverse are in the following order: middle: the Epiphany; above: the Annunciation; left and right: the Evangelists; below: the Visitation.

Reverse: middle: the Crucifixion; above: the Resurrection; left and right: the Evangelists; below: the Transfiguration.

A particle of the Holy Cross is built into this piece. The Belgrade Metropolitan, Ilarion, presented the cross to the Community of the monastery Krušedol. From this and the other gifts he donated to churches and monasteries, one can infer that he was a man of discrimination who commissioned only top masters for manufacturing his presents.

Museum of the Serbian Orthodox Church, Belgrade
Literature: L. Mirković, *The Antiquities of the monasteries of Fruška Gora,* (Belgrade 1931) p. 31.

73 Cross
1654
Silver; enamel, silver-gilt
Height: 520 mm   Width 200 mm
Made for the monastery of Hopovo, Serbia.

An orthodox cross set on a baroque foot in the form of a six-petalled flower. The foot is profiled, and decorated with rosettes and stereotyped figures of saints. An enamelled knop is set in the middle of its short handle. The cross is of Baroque type, branchy, with two stylized dragons on the sides guarding it and three crowns on its three free arms. The Sun and the Moon are set on its horizontal arms. The wooden part of the cross bears representations of the twelve great Holidays. The cross is encircled with small decorative medallions with half-figures of saints.

The silver mounting of this piece is completely subordinate to the wooden parts.

The foot bears an inscription about the founder Hieromonk Ilija (Elijah) and the Master Nedeljko of Ćiprovac. In the mid 17th century, the workshops of Ćiprovac began the use of wire enamel and among the first to adopt this technique was Nedeljko. The goldsmiths' work of Dubrovnik exerted a decisive influence on Ćiprovac's craftsmen in this case, for, besides the enamelling technique, it also transmitted the Baroque elements.

It is not unusual that a synthesis of various elements (Serbian, Turkish, Baroque), combined with many different techniques and materials, brings about the creation of successful works of art like this one.

Museum of the Serbian Orthodox Church, Belgrade
Literature: B. Radojković, (1966) pp. 147–9; L. Mirković, (1931) p. 57.

74 Cross

17th–18th century
Silver-gilt; enamel, turquoise, cut glass, carved wood
Height: 230 mm   Width: 95 mm   Depth: 13 mm
Bought from the Jakšićs of Pljevlja, Montenegro.

Set on a convex foot which grows into a simple handle (round in
section) with a circular knop in the middle. Its lower arm is
longer than the other three, ending in trefoils. The silver mounts
are decorated with plant ornament and interlace and the whole
surface is inlaid with light- and dark-green enamel.

The cross bears an arrangement of settings in the form of
flowers with turquoises and ruby-like cabochon glass. It is also
decorated with many pearls. The baroque elements are noticeable on the foot and knop.

Judging by the elaboration and style of the enamel on the
mounts, it comes from the same workshop where the cross of
Nedeljko of Ćiprovac was made.

The wooden part is older and dates from the mid 17th century.
It is clear that this cross is the work of a good master who tried by
perforation to create an illusion of spatial depth in the landscape
and architecture. The scenes represented on the cross are placed
under Saracenic arches. Obverse, centre: the Baptism with four
participants; above: a device; left and right: a cherub; above and
beneath: an Evangelist with no attributes for identification.

Reverse, centre: the Crucifixion; above: a device; left and
right: a cherub; above and below: an Evangelist.

Inv. No. 783, Museum of Applied Art, Belgrade
Literature: B. Radojković, '16th and 17th Century enamelled
Crosses.' *Zbornik of the Museum of Applied Art,* I, (Belgrade 1955)
pp. 81, 82.

74

75 Censer
Early 16th century
Cast silver; open work, chased, silver-gilt
Height: 360 mm   Height of the lid: 130 mm
Made for the monastery of Sveta Trojica (Trinity) near Pljevlja, Montenegro.

Set on a hexagonal convex foot decorated with the open work plant motifs, and narrowing upwards.

Composed of a hemisphere (the incense and ember container) and a lid in the form of a round Gothic tower. The tower is decorated with Gothic windows with quatrefoils, rosettes and pilasters, and with birds and animals.

The censer ends in an undecorated conical turret with a big cross finial. It hangs on five thick plaited chains with balls, small round bells, and crosses.

Made under the influence of Rumanian Gothic, if not actually in Rumania.

At that time, Rumanian goldsmiths were influenced by German Gothic and, simultaneously, via Serbia, by Dubrovnik goldsmiths' work. Serbia and Rumania enjoyed close relations with each other.

Treasury of the monastery of Sveta Trojica (Trinity) near Pljevlja
Literature: B. Radojković, (1966) pp. 92–93.

76 Censer
1591
Cast silver; open work, chased, silver-gilt
Height: 340 mm   Length of chains: 700 mm
Made for the monastery of Studenica.

The foot is hexafoil, convex, profiled and narrowing towards its upper part. There are small open work arcades on the base. The incense container is decorated with ribbed ornament. The lid is in the form of a conical Gothic tower in four parts, and it is decorated with quatrefoils and rosettes.

Pilasters with finials are between the windows. The censer hangs on five chains connected to the body by springs, the upper part of the chains ends in a four-sided canopy.

This type of censer used in the Eastern Orthodox liturgy originated in the Central European, and especially the German, workshops, whose influence was transmitted to the Balkans down the Danube trade routes.

At the time of this censer's manufacture, Serbian goldsmiths' work was also strongly influenced by the Rumanian master goldsmiths inspired by late Gothic architecture.

Treasury of the monastery of Studenica
Literature: B. Radojković, (1966) pp.93–4.

77 Censer
1617
Cast silver; open work
Height: 270 mm   Width: 110 mm
Made for the Temple of the Beheading of St. John the Baptist (Hram Usekovanja Jovana Preteče), at Orakhovica, Slavonia.

A shallow incense and ember container is set on a profiled hexafoil convex foot. The foot is decorated with open work arcades and an inscription. Profiled fretwork ribs go vertically over the container. The lid is cast in the form of a cone, reminding one of Gothic towers. The quatrefoil and bifoil finials are executed by perforation. The protruding profiled gables bear birds. The upper part of the censer ends with a turret with a ball as the finial, and hangs on five plaited chains with small round bells and a round canopy on top.

When one compares this censer with those made by Avramije Hlapović, it is clear that it is also his work, although it bears no maker's mark. This censer is very similar to other liturgical objects of that time which come from the cultural circle which had Avramije Hlapović as one of its central figures.

Treasury of the monastery of Orakhovica
Literature: B. Radojković, (1966) p. 127.

78 Censer
First half of 17th century
Cast silver; wrought, chased
Height: 260 mm   Length: 450 mm
Made for the monastery of Savina.

Composed of an incense and ember cup and handle; the handle is a level tablet with a slightly protruding moulding along the edge. It is engraved with the figure of the Archdeacon Stefan in his ornate vestments with an archidiaconal stole, a censer in his right hand and a book in his left. Beside it is inscribed, 'Archdeacon Stefan', and at the end of the handle, the maker's initials. The handle is supported by a narrow cylinder.

The ember cup is set on a profiled hexafoil foot, also engraved, ending with a garland of Gothic plant motifs. The rim of the cup is ornamented with a larger garland of the same motifs. The lid is in the form of a dome with six turrets along the edge, and a larger one in the centre. The turrets are four-sided; the central turret six-sided, and they all end with crosses with beads at the ends of their arms.

This censer is not overloaded with the decorative motifs of a late Gothic which is already considerably Islamicised, but its elements are harmoniously balanced.

Treasury of the monastery of Savina
Literature: B. Radjković, (1966) pp. 93, 125–6.

79 Hand Censer
1654
Cast silver; chased
Height: 290 mm   Width: 270 mm
Made for the monastery of Nova Vinča, Mt. Fruška Gora.

This is a characteristic example of a hand censer. The handle is level, in the form of a stylized leaf, with a large inscription and an arched composition representing the Purification of the Virgin Mary in the Temple. Along the edge of the handle goes a small moulding of Gothic trefoils. The handle ends with a griffon's head.

The lid is in the form of a complex polygonal Gothic edifice with quatrefoils, rosettes and small profiled columns.

Censers of the hand type were used in the Eastern Orthodox liturgies, especially in monastic churches. They originated on Mouth Athos and were used there during the evening prayers of the monks. Throughout the Middle Ages they bore the characteristics of Byzantine art, and later absorbed (from the early 17th century) some Gothic elements.

In the mid-17th century, a new variant appeared: the lid of the censer became elongated and wider, most often becoming a three storeyed dome, imitating the complex architecture of Gothic towers. The influence of Rumanian goldsmiths' work is noticeable in this piece.

Museum of the Serbian Orthodox Church, Belgrade
Literature: (1966) p. 126.

80 Icon Lamp
Early 17th century
Cast silver; open work, chased
Height: 130 mm   Width of the opening: 85 mm
Find from Studenica, Serbia.

In the form of a truncated cone; composed of three soldered-on vertical perforated tablets, horizontally intersected by three wreaths of stylized lotus flowers. The upper zone is horizontally divided into three friezes: two cherubs in the biforms of the first frieze; medallions with trefoils in the middle frieze, and two pairs of seated saints in the biforms of the third frieze. The lower zone, too, has three friezes: the first, with half-figures of cherubs in square medallions; the second, beneath, with chalices and intertwined plant ornament; the lowest with sitting figures of saints in the arcades. The handles are in the form of stylized branchlets.

This piece reflects a mixture of late Byzantine and late Gothic influences together with the Baroque.

Inv. No. 3165, Museum of Applied Art, Belgrade.

80

81 Icon Lamp
Early 17th century
Cast bronze; open work, chased, gilt
Height with chains: 640 mm   Width of opening: 96 mm
Unearthed at the monastery of Zrze, Macedonia.

In the form of a truncated cone with its narrower part turned downwards. Vertically divided into three fields, with the following compositions: a Deisis intertwined with vines; St. George, mounted, slaying the dragon; and in a round medallion, the Virgin *Orans* with a two-headed eagle below, and in the lowest zone, half-figures of St. Theodore and St. Nicholas.

The icon lamp hangs on three chains fixed by loops to its body, and conjoined at the top.

Stylistic analysis of this piece reveals its profound relationship with late Byzantine models and those once brought to Serbia by the Turks. Islamic influences are noticeable in the treatment of the arches as well as in the vines.

Icon lamps of this type were manufactured at that time in the northern part of Greece and on Mount Athos.

Inv. No. 1153, Museum of Applied Art, Belgrade
Literature: B. Radojković, (1956) Cat. No. 340.

82 Chalice
16th century
Cast silver; open-work, embossed, chased; silver-gilt
Height: 240 mm   Width: 145 mm
Made for the monastery of Krušedol, Mt. Fruška Gora.

From a six-foil base there rises a small profiled foot with a spherical knot with six lobes separated from one another by a twisted band. The knot is decorated with saints' figures. The cup bears open-work ornament and its six applied medallions are filled with braid motifs.

The chalice belongs to the Central European variant of the late Gothic style. The ornamentation also reveals strong Renaissance influence.

Museum of the Serbian Orthodox Church, Belgrade
Literature: B. Radojković, (1956) Cat. No. 281; ibid., (1966) pp. 100, 123.

83 Chalice
1568
Silver; embossed, chiselled; silver-gilt
Height: 275 mm   Width of the base: 170 mm
From the monastery of Dečani, Kosovo.

A deep cup with a profiled hexafoil foot narrowing into an elegant stem with a knot. The foot decorated with stylized chick-pea stems and medallions corresponding to arabesques. The lower zone of the cup is encircled by two bands of chased lilies.

Particularly interesting is a round plaque under the cup, richly decorated with chick-pea branchlets and flowers in blue, green, white and vermilion enamel. The fine execution and clear colours are reminiscent of the most beautiful pieces of the Iznik faience which undoubedly exerted a strong influence on Serbian enamellers. This chalice is, more than any other, a synthesis of oriental and western influences in its form and ornament. The form is completely western: for example, it closely resembles the chalice held by John the Evangelist in the sculpture by Baccio da Montelupo of Bologna, while the decorative motifs are, in origin, Turkish.

The chalice was made by order of Radivoje, probably a Christian *spakhia,* for the monastery of Dečani.

Treasury of the monastery of Dečani
Literature: B. Radojković, (1966) p. 152.

83

84 Chalice
1579

Cast silver; embossed, chased; silver-gilt, and set with stones.
Diameter of the foot 190 mm   Diameter of the brim 130 mm
Made for the monastery of Sveta Trojica (Trinity) near Pljevlja,
Montenegro.

The foot is trilobed, convex, and profiled, with lattice and ribbed
ornament. Decorated with multicoloured semiprecious stones
and chased with intertwining branchlets and leaves. Above the
foot, where the stem begins, glitters a six-foil rosette with stones.
The stem (hexagonal in section) is profiled and also decorated
with stones; the knop is segmented. The cup is deep, the upper
part in the form of a flower ending in a band embossed with
Gothic trefoils. An inscription is engraved around the of the cup.
  Chalices of this type with individual variations in ornament
are typologically linked with the Herzegovinian school of goldsmiths' work. The Gothic form of the chalice derives from Italy
via the Adriatic Coast.
  The chalice was made for the monastery of Sveta Trojica in
1579 by order of the Prior Hieromonk Stefan.

The monastery of Sveta Trojica near Pljevlja
Literature: B. Radojković, (1966) p. 122.

85 Ripida Icons (a pair of)
1559–60

Silver and gold alloy; wrought, chiselled
Width: 336 mm   Length of handle: 465 mm
Made for the monastery of Banja.

A Turkish rosette in the centre, with six-winged seraphs in the
round medallions encircling it. A circular band of intertwined
branchlets separates the other two bands work with a fine
inscription. The handles also bear a spiralling inscription.
  This pair of *ripida* icons show how strong the influence of
Turco-Persian art was in Serbia and to what an extent it succeeded in ousting figurative in favour of ornamental decoration.
  The inscription refers to the commissioning of this piece for
the monastery of Banja, and to its founder Makarije, the Metropolitan of Peć and of all Serbia.

Treasury of the monastery of Banja
Literature: D. Milošević, (1980) Cat. No. 114; M. Sakota, (Belgrade
1981) pp. 39–46.

86 Ripida Icons

1570
Silver; engraved, chased and silver-gilt
Width: 270 mm   Length of handle 170 mm
Made for the monastery of Dečani, Kosovo.

These icons show the Divine Liturgy. On the first icon is, on one side, the Great Pilgrimage with the Virgin *Eleusa* in the centre, and, on the other, Jesus Christ as an Angel.

The second icon represents the Baptism of the Apostles with Jesus Christ as an Archpriest, on one side, and a six-winged Seraph on the other.

The compositions closely resemble contemporary fresco painting.

The innovations introduced by the goldsmith Kondo Vuk are the decorative motifs which originate in Turco-Persian art (the chick-pea shoot with small roses, peach flowers). Even some details of the figures reflect the influence of miniature painting. The costume details are contemporary.

This pair of *ripida* icons by Kondo Vuk rank among the most valuable pieces of Serbian goldsmiths' work because of their uniqueness, their fine execution, and the artist's subtle use of material and techniques. It could only have been made in one of the Kosovo-Metrokhian workshops, near the monastery of Dečani, where all the dominant artistic influences in Serbia intertwined in the most beautiful way.

The artist was commissioned to make this pair of icons in 1570 by the *spakhia*, Radivoj, who donated it to the Monastery.

Treasury of the monastery Dečani
Literature: Dj. Bošković, V. Petković, *The monastery of Dečani,* (Belgrade 1941) p. 9; B. Radojković, (1966) pp. 110–11.

No. 1   Obverse

No. 1 Reverse

No. 2 Reverse

87 Icon (a single *ripida*)
1664
Silver; embossed; filigree, silver-gilt
Width: 310 mm
Made for the monastery of Krušedol, Mt. Fruška Gora.

In a circle in the centre of the icon is depicted the Annunciation with standing figures. The background of the composition is filled with architecture. An Archangel holds a lily, and the Virgin Mary holds yarn and a spindle. They are encircled by elliptical medallions bearing figures of saints, the Prophets, six-winged seraphs, and cherubs. On the other side, in a six-point star, stands the figure of Jesus Christ the *Pantocrator,* encircled, as on the first side, with medallions. Cherubs and seraphs are set in the angles between the points of the star.

A band of stylized enamel plant ornament with filigree flows along the edges of both sides. The icon has no maker's mark, but it is the work of one of the masters of Ćiprovac and it can certainly be attributed to one of the first ranking artists. Ćiprovac was a great goldsmithing centre which resisted the influence of indigenous folk art, and avoided the stagnation which took place in most Serbian centres of production. The icon was donated to the monastery of Krušedol by Ilarion, the Metropolitan of Belgrade, in 1664.

Museum of the Serbian Orthodox Church, Belgrade
Literature: B. Radojković, (1966) pp. 150–151.

88 Icon Shrine (for keeping pectoral pendants)
1652
Silver; filigree, enamel; carved wood
Height: 65 mm   Width 50 mm
Donated to the monastery of Krušedol.

In the form of a square silver box, with two carved wooden icons inside. The Virgin and Child is depicted in the centre on the left side. Around her, in rectangular arcades, are half-figures of the Prophets. The arcades are mounted and decorated with filigree and stones. In the centre on the right side is the Holy Trinity; in the corners, the Evangelists, with saints around them.

The wood-carver, Master Lezar's, endeavour to give individual traits to the figures distinguishes this work from all the others of this type.

The shrine is dated 1652 and was donated to the monastery of Krušedol by the Metropolitan Belgrade and Srem Haji-Ilarion.

Museum of the Serbian Orthodox Church, Belgrade
Literature: B. Radojković, (Belgrade 1977) p. 24.

89 Icon Shrine
1664
Silver; gold; diamonds; carved wood
Width: 140 mm
Donated to the monastery of Krušedol.

In the form of a round box with a lid, and with two carved round icons. The surface of the silver box is decorated with filigree, light- and dark-green, and dark-blue enamel, and stones. Our Lady *Platytera* with Seraphs is depicted in the centre of the left-hand icon, encircled by two lines of half-figure angels, saints and the Prophets intertwined with vines. The tree of Jesse is shown beneath. The Holy Trinity (Abraham and the Three Angels) is depicted on the right hand icon. The scene is represented against a rich architectural background. Around it are medallions with saints; above two angels with a *mandorla* and a gold cross containing a particle of the Holy Cross.

This icon shrine was made on Mount Athos and it ranks among the most beautiful pieces of the kind. The inscription along the edge says that it was donated to the monastery of Krušedol by Haji-Ilarion, the Metropolitan of Belgrade and Srem in 1664.

Museum of the Serbian Orthodox Church, Belgrade
Literature: L. Mirković, (1931) pp. 35–6; B. Radojković, (1977) pp. 33–4.

90 Icon Shrine
End of 17th–early 18th century
Cast silver; wrought, chased; filigree
Height: 81 mm   Width: 83 mm
Bought from a private owner by the Museum of Applied Art, Belgrade, in 1977.

The box is rectangular, almost square, edged with bands of pseudo-filigree and dotted ornament. One side chased with a large decorative motif of intertwined vines, leaves and two snakes' heads, reminiscent of the complex initials in 14th century Serbian manuscripts. Stylized trefoils in the corners. Mild

Baroque influence is felt here. The other side of the box repousse with a decorative motif composed of Baroque plant and architectural elements. Two carved wood icons set inside under small tablets decorated with plant motifs in filigree and perforated in the form of sixteen-sided medallions. The tablets framing the icons look as though they have been prepared for enamelling which, for some reason, was not executed.

The icon on the left is horizontally divided into two fields. The lower zone, to the left, shows the standing figure of St. Haralampius with a book in his left hand, blessing with the right. A seated St. Mark with a scroll on his knees is on the right. Between the two saints is a one-legged table with a winged lion and an inkstand on it. The upper zone shows the Annunciation. Both scenes are represented against a rich architectural landscape with almost sculptural buildings. The icon on the right side represents SS. George and Dimitri, mounted and confronted, in characteric poses. Between them, in the *mandorla,* stands the figure of Jesus Christ.

Both scenes are executed in the Levantine Baroque style while the work of the goldsmith is completely subordinate to that of the wood-carver. The mediocrity and lack of inventiveness noticeable on the box are fully made up for by the meticulous work done by the carver who was a master of small-scale sculptural detail.

This piece illustrates the declining Serbian goldsmiths' craft.

Inv. No. 9796, Museum of Applied Art, Belgrade
Literature: B. Radojković, (1977) Cat. No. 71.

91 **Wafer Vessels** (a set of)
1637
Cast silver; open-work, embossed; silver-gilt
Height: 300 mm   Width: 380 mm
Made for the monastery of Studenica.

Four cups with feet, conical lids and cross finials set on a round plate. The cups are made in the Gothic manner with quatrefoils, rosettes and frontons. A *trichirion* cup is also set on the plate. Along the rim flows an inscription about the Master Ivan and the donors, Dionysius and Gregory.

An analysis of the Eucharist wafer vessels of the monastery of Dečani leads one to suppose that this set represents a later work by the same master, Ivan (Milić) of Cajniče.

Treasury of the monastery of Studenica
Literature: B. Radojković, (1966) p. 139.

92 **Wafer Vessels** (a set of)
1648
Silver; embossed, chased
Height: 280 mm   Width of the plate 250 mm
Made for monastery of Krušedol, Mt. Fruška Gora.

Set on three profiled legs narrowing upwards, each with a knop in the middle. The shallow plate bears three cups with nodules and conical lids with cross finials. The cups are made in open-work of richly intertwined vines. A small *trichirion* cup is also set on the plate in the centre of which stands a smaller plate with a foot and tiny enclosure around the rim. An inscription flows along the brim.

It was ordered from Belgrade by the Hieromonk Ignatius through the mediation of the Hieromonk Joachim, and donated to the monastery of Krušedol.

Museum of the Serbian Orthodox Church, Belgrade
Literature: B. Radojković, (1956) Cat. No. 325.

93 **Wafer Vessels** (a set of)
1652
Cast silver; open-work, embossed; wire enamel
Height: 420 mm   Width of the plate: 250 mm
Made for the monastery of Tvrdoš, Herzegovina.

The round base with a decorative motif of vines, bears a large shallow plate in the centre of which stands a tall container of icon-lamp type with an angel finial. A tiny low border composed of trefoils encircles the plate near the rim. An inscription is chased around the rim.

Four branches, bearing two smaller ewer-shaped vessels and two pans, extend upwards from the central container, which is decorated with scenes from the New Testament. The lids of the central container and the ewers are decorated with enamel. The finial, a Renaissance angel, is the sole example of this type of treatment in Serbian goldsmiths' work, and the mould for it probably came into the Master Neško's hands from the Adriatic Coast.

This piece is the most mature work of Neško Prolimleković. He was technically very skilful, and eclectic in composing his decorative motifs with enamel, Gothic and Turkish elements.

This set of wafer vessels was made in 1652 for the monastery of Tvrdoš by order of the Hieromonk Evgenije (Eugene).

Treasury of the monastery Savina
Literature: B. Radojković, (1966) p. 137.

94 Wafer Vessels
Circa 1670
Cast silver; open-work, embossed, chased
Height: 320 mm   Width of the plate 350 mm
Made for the monastery of Dečani, Kosovo.

Four cups on legs with knops stand on a shallow plate with a profiled rim. A *trichirion* vessel in the centre.

The cups consist of two parts, one part with quatrefoils, rosettes and frontons, the other, a conical lid with a cross finial. The lids are engraved with cypresses inlaid with fish-scale ornament. The small *trichirion* cups are shaped like tulips with finials. This set of wafer vessels was made either in 1663 or 1670 (it is difficult to say precisely, because the inscription is damaged) at the time of the Prior Christopher.

A comparative analysis leads one to conclude that this unmarked piece is the work of Ivan Milić of Cajniče. A number of his works has survived to this day, enough to reflect most of the virtues and shortcomings of 17th-century Serbian goldsmiths' work, in general. Ivan Milić was known for his prolific production of Church articles, and, therefore, in addition to his own workshop, he must have had many collaborators. He had his own moulds, and to some extent, went in for an early form of mass production.

Treasury of the monastery Dečani
Literature: B. Radojković, (1966) pp. 139–140.

95 Four-volume Gospel Setting
1559
Silver; embossed; silver-gilt
Height: 450 mm   Width: 290 mm
Made for the monastery Krušedol, Mt. Fruška Gora.

Obverse: the Crucifixion in low relief. To the right of Jesus Christ stands Mary supported by a woman; to the left, a meditative John the Divine with Longinus carrying shield and spear. Beneath the Cross is Adam's skull, and above it two angels, the Sun and the Moon. Portraits of the Apostles, one above another, are along the vertical sides of the mount. In the corners, the seated figures of the Evangelists. Above Jesus Christ, a stereotyped portrait of the Bishop Maxim described in the inscription as Despot Stefan. The rest of the space all covered with stylized vines intertwined with flowers, chick-pea leaves and inscriptions.

Reverse: the Resurrection in the variant of the Christ's Descent into Hell.

This is the first surviving setting after the Okhrid piece to be made in the territory of Serbia, and it was executed in memory of Bishop Maxim by order of Prior Silvester. The artist found the model for his Crucifixion scene in 14th-century icon- and miniature-painting as well as in the icons of Italo-Cretan origin dating either from the 14th or the first quarter of the 16th century. The parallels for the Descent into Hell are in contemporary painting.

Among the goldsmiths of the 16th century Master Petar Smederevac of Bečkerek has a special place. His freedom of composition, excellent figurative fore-shortening, the individualization of his characters, his sense of drama and exquisite stylization caused him to influence the whole Bečkerek school of goldsmiths' work.

Museum of the Serbian Orthodox Church, Belgrade
Literature: B. Radojković (1956) Cat. No. 272; ibid., (1966) pp. 105–108.

96 Four-volume Gospel Setting
Second half of the 16th century
Silver; chased; silver-gilt
Height: 330 mm   Width 190 mm
Made for the Old Serbian Church in Sarajevo, Bosnia and Herzegovina.

Obverse: above: the Crucifixion with Mary and John. Below: a half-figure of the Archangel Michael. The first words of each of the four Gospels chased in a wide band around the edges. The symbols of the Evangelists engraved in medallions on the corners. Around the Crucifixion spreads a vine intertwined with chick-pea leaves, similar to that on the Gospel mounting from the monastery of Trojica (Trinity) of Pljevla.

Reverse: the Virgin & Child, enthroned, with two angels beside her. The treatment of the figures and surfaces imitates 13th–14th century models. In its simplicity and graphic quality this setting is reminiscent of an engraving. Indeed it was probably made after a wood-cut or engraving, not an uncommon practice, in the 15th and 16th centuries.

The development of printing in Belgrade (the first printing shop was founded in 1552), and its undoubted influence on the goldsmiths' trade which flourished there, as well as the many orders for the Old Serbian Church in Sarajevo by well-off

Bosnian tradesmen and merchants, support the possibility that this Gospel setting is also a work by Belgrade craftsmen.

Old Serbian Church, Sarajevo
Literature: L. Mirković, 'The Antiquities of the Old Serbian Church in Sarajevo,' *Spomenik,* XXXV, p. 22; B. Radojković, '16th and 17th Century Serbian Gospel Mounts,' *Zbornik of the Museum of Applied Art,* III–IV, (Belgrade 1958) pp. 54–55; ibid., (1966).

97 Four-volume Gospel Setting

Second half of the 16th century
Cast silver; open-work, chased, embossed; silver-gilt
Height: 420 mm   Width: 330 mm
Made for the monastery of Sv. Trojica of Pljevlja, Serbia.

Obverse: a cast scene of the Christ's Descent into Hell. In the corners, on rectangular tablets, the standing figures of the Evangelists. Between them four tablets inscribed with the first words from each of the four Gospels. Along the sides flows a wide openwork intertwined stem with chick-pea leaves of Turkish origin filled with niello. The iconographical innovations (for example, the Christ in a *mandorla*) shown in the Descent into Hell reflect the italianate icons of the first half of the 16th century.

Reverse: decorated with plates and small tablets executed under the influence of Turco-Persian art, merely for the sake of ornamentation. A later binder, Eustatius, put his signature on the setting in a secret inscription in the 17th century.

The plates on the front side are identical with the central one on the *Tetraevangelion* from the monastery of Piva, a plaque with an Evangelist on the book mount from the Old Serbian Church in Sarajevo, and also with the plates from a lost *Tetraevangelion* kept in the Museum of Applied Art in Belgrade. These pieces are all the work of a Herzegovinian artist about whom we do not have any more detailed information. This mounting was specially made for the monastery of Sveta Trojica of Pljevlja.

The monastery of Sveta Trojica of Pljevlja
Literature: Dr. S. Radojčić, *Old Serbian Miniatures,* (Belgrade 1950) p. 57; B. Radojković (1966) pp. 118, 120, 123.

98 Gospel Setting

1556–7
Silver; embossed; silver-gilt
Height: 430 mm   Width: 260 mm   Diameter: 84 mm
Made for the monastery of Vitovnica, Kučaq.

Obverse: Christ's Twelve Holy Days separated from one another by arcading. Reverse: the Death and Assumption of the Virgin according to the apocryphal sources. This representation of the Death of the Virgin is one of the oldest to be found on book mounts. In general this piece is very interesting because it reflects the many diverse influences under which the artist worked: the old icons, the decoration found in miniatures and embroidery and the contemporary graphic arts. The immediate source of all these influences may have been the big Treasury and Library of the monastery of Dečani, the focal point at that time of all the cultural influences spreading over the Balkans.

Kondo Vuk, the goldsmith, solves the spatial problems in his compositions in a new way, despite his use of old iconographic models to represent the Death of the Virgin. The nearest parallel for such a solution is found in the icon the Death of the Virgin by the Italian painter, Andrea Rico da Candia, painted around 1498.

Museum of the Serbian Orthodox Church, Belgrade
Literature: B. Radojković, (1966) pp. 110–115.

98
(detail)

99   Gospel Setting

Circa 1580

Cast silver; chased, embossed; silver-gilt
Central plate: Height: 165 mm   Width: 140 mm
Corner tablets: Height: 90 mm   Width: 45 mm
Provenance unknown.

The central plate shows the Resurrection in the Descent into Hell
variant. The small corner tablets are ornamented with standing
figures of the Evangelists. These parts are identical in size and
style with the plates on the Gospel setting from the monastery of
Sveta Trojica of Pljevlja; the central plate on the Gospel setting
from the monastery of Piva; and the plaque on the book setting
from the Old Serbian Church in Sarajevo.

All these pieces were made in the same Herzegovinian
workshop and cast in the same moulds. They represent some of
the best creations of 16th century Herzegovinian goldsmiths.

Inv. No. 7021, Museum of Applied Art, Belgrade
Literature: B. Radojković, 'Three Book Settings made by Serbian
Goldsmiths in the 16th, 17th, and 18th centuries,' *Zbornik of the
Museum of Applied Art,* XIII, (Belgrade 1969) pp. 75, 78.

100   Four-volume Gospel Setting

1630

Silver; embossed
Height: 308 mm   Width: 205 mm   Diameter: 60 mm
Made for the monastery of Mt. Fruška Gora.

Obverse: the Deisis in the upper part, and four Serbian saints in
the lower. Jesus is Christ enthroned, the Virgin *Paraklesis* to the
left, and John the Baptist, to the right. This composition is derived
from 16th and 17th century icons.

Reverse: the Ascension. The artist brought variations into this
composition derived from miniatures of Syrian origin and frescoes from the Patriarchate of Peć.

This is by Neško Prolimleković. All his works have the characteristics of very expressive drawing, naïve proportions and
deformed shapes, and an extraordinary mastery of ornament.
His qualities are typical of 16th century goldsmiths' work in
Serbia.

Museum of the Serbian Orthodox Church, Belgrade
Literature: B. Radojković, (1958) pp. 59, 61; ibid., (1966) pp.
136–137.

Central plaque

Corner plaque

Corner plaque

101 Four-volume Gospel Setting
1644
Silver; embossed; silver-gilt
Height: 380 mm   Width: 220 mm
From the monastery of Dečani, Kosovo.

Obverse: the Deisis with Jesus Christ enthroned, in low relief.
The composition can be directly paralleled in 12th and 13th
century miniatures, but also in contemporary painting.
    Reverse: the Ascension of Jesus Christ in a *mandorla* carried by
angels; beneath, the Virgin with the Apostles and Archangels.
    The model used for this composition is in the Church of the
Holy Apostles at the Patriarchate of Peć.
    This is attributed to Prolimleković on the basis of an icono-
logical analysis.
    Unlike the Hopovo *tetraevangelion* setting, this shows a quite
different treatment of the figures: they are now more sculptural,
and freer in their stance and their vestments are more richly
draped. Notwithstanding the well-chosen iconographical
themes, the artist obviously suffers from a lack of anatomical
knowledge and the technique of figurative foreshortening, in
common with the majority of Serbian goldsmiths of the 17th
century, when ornament flourished at the expense of the figures
and composition.
    This gospel setting was ordered in 1644 by the monk
Centirion for the monastery of Dečani.

Treasury of the monastery of Dečani.
Literature: B. Radojković, (1958) pp. 60, 81; ibid., (1966)
pp. 136–7.

102 Gospel Setting
1656
Cast silver; open work, chased; silver-gilt
Height: 335 mm   Width 215 mm
Made for the monastery of Krušedol, Mt. Fruška Gora.

Only the obverse has survived. The Crucifixion is in the centre
with four medallions with the Apostles on each side, square
tablets with the Evangelists in the corners, cast seraphs above
and beneath the Crucifixion, a reduced scene of the Christ's
Ascension, above, and the Archangel Michael below. The tablets
are separated from one another by the open-work bands of
trefoils.

It is obvious that the model used for this piece was a printed
illustration, probably one of Italian origin. This and the type of
the ornamental band suggest that this piece was made in a
Belgrade workshop.

Inv. No. 178, Museum of the Serbian Orthodox Church,
Belgrade
Literature: B. Radojković, (1966) p. 113.

103 Four-volume Gospel Setting
1657
Cast silver; embossed; silver-gilt
Height: 340 mm   Width: 205 mm
Made for the monastery of Tvrdoš; until 1694 kept in the
monastery of Trebinje, and then moved to the monastery of
Savina, Montenegro.

Obverse: two zones with a rope border, the upper zone bearing a
representation of the Virgin and two women (right), and St. John
the Divine with Longinus (left). Beneath: the Ascension, in the
Descent into Hell variant. Bottom: an inscription about the
donor. Along the vertical edges flows a tiny vine with leaves and
bunches of grapes composing medallions decorated with half-
figures of the Apostles, illustrating the text: 'I am a vine . . .'
    Reverse: the Death of the Virgin; above: the Assumption; top:
the Virgin in a *mandorla* with two angels; bottom: the maker's
inscription. Along the vertical edges, a band of vineleaf ornament forming twelve medallions with half-figures of the Prophets illustrating the text: 'Thou werst foreshadowed by the
Prophets . . .' This setting was executed by two masters; the front
by an unidentified artist, the back by Mihajlo Trebinjac. The
whole is in the spirit of the new pictorial concepts of the period.
The front is reminiscent of Italo-Cretan icons, while the reverse
is very similar to the painting of the Death of the Virgin by the
Italian, Andrea Rico da Candia. The ornament is a combination
of Byzantine and Italian Renaissance motifs. The influence of
the Italian Renaissance came via Dalmatia into the province of
Herzegovina where this piece originated.

The monastery of Savina
Literature: B. Radojković, (1956) Cat. No. 405; ibid., (1966) pp.
119–120.

104 Gospel Setting
1661–2
Cast silver; open-work; chased
Height: 290 mm   Width: 205 mm   Depth: 75 mm
Remodelled for the monastery of Hopovo, Mt. Fruška Gora.

Composed of several perforated small plates brought together
by a twisted vine.

In the middle of the upper zone stands a *panagia,* a pectoral
icon of the Virgin. Left and right: the Archangels Michael and
Gabriel. In the middle of the central zone: St. George on horse-
back; left and right: the Apostles Peter and Paul. In the middle of
the lower zone, in a double arcade: two Serbian saints, and two
more (left and right). They probably represent portraits of
Serbian rulers, probably the last Brankovićs. The text about the
maker is underneath. Along the edges of the setting winds a
perforated stem set with multicoloured precious stones.

It is noticeable here that the artist used a variety of moulds
inherited from Bečkerek's workshops. Apart from the *panagia* of
the Virgin and the two Apostles, the rest reflect the eclipse of a
once great art. The naïveté and lack of both anatomical knowledge
and iconographical coherence indicate the decadence of the
once important goldsmithing centre, Bečkerek.

The inscription records that the Gospel setting was remodelled
for the monastery of Hopovo by the master Vuk, in Bečkerek.

Museum of the Serbian Orthodox Church, Belgrade
Literature: B. Radojković, (1966) pp. 109–110.

105 Reliquary
1550–51
Cast silver; open-work, embossed
Height: 365 mm   Width: 200 mm   Depth: 80 mm
Made for the monastery of Sišatovac.

In the form of a five-domed church. Richly decorated with
architectural details and with portraits of the Prophet Hermits
and Holy Warriors embossed on the sides of the church. This
reliquary made by Dmitar of Lipova is one of the first Serbian
ones to be made in the form of a church. It is identical to the
reliquary from the monastery of St. Catherine in the Sinai
Peninsula.

It is a combination of the traditional, the Romanesque-Gothic,
and Arabic elements. The maker, Master Jevrem, is skilled in the
definition of architecture and architectural details, but far weaker
in the execution of figures.

The reliquary was made by order of the monks Theophilus
and Ilarion of the monastery of Sišatovac.

Museum of the Serbian Orthodox Church, Belgrade
Literature: B. Radojković, 'The Reliquary of Dmitar of Lipova,' *Rad
vojvodjanskih muzeja,* V (1956); ibid., (1966) pp. 115–117.

106 Reliquary
Second half of 1573
Silver and gold alloy; cast, engraved
Height: 300 mm   Length: 227 mm
Made for the monastery of Banja, Serbia.

Square decorated with bands of plant ornament, and set on four
stylized small legs. An inscription flows along the edges of the
box. The lid, in the form of a two-sided roof, is fixed to the box
with hinges.

Three cupolas with Gothic drums are set in the middle of the
roof. The hexagonal drums bear quatrefoils, rosettes, frontons,
profiled pilasters and supports. The turrets above the drums are
conical and smooth, with finials (balls and crosses). Stylistically,
this reliquary is nearest to the reliquary from the monastery of
Papraća (1586).

Treasury of the monastery Banja, near Priboj
Literature: D. Milošević, (1980) Cat. No. 117; M. Sakota, (Belgrade
1981) pp. 46–51.

105

107 Reliquary
1586
Cast silver; wrought; parcel-gilt
Height: 210 mm   Length: 190 mm   Width: 90 mm
Formerly the property of the monastery of Papraća, acquired
and donated to the Old Orthodox Church in Sarajevo, Bosnia.

In the form of an edifice with a two-sided roof bearing three
cupolas. The cupolas are conical with hexagonal drums and
Gothic open-work around their bases. The longer sides of the
roof have three gables each, and the narrower, one each. Along
the upper and lower edges of the reliquary flow bands of
ornament, and two inscriptions encircle it: the first refers to the
donors, Prior Zachariah and Monk Longinus; the second says
that the reliquary was acquired and donated by the Priest Jovan
(John) to the Serbian Church in Sarajevo.
   This type of reliquary represents a transitional type, evolving
towards the type of reliquary made in the early 17th century. In
the combination of Turkish ornament and Gothic motifs, and in
its technical details it is reminiscent of work made in the workshop of Hlapović.

Serbian Orthodox Church, Sarajevo
Literature: B. Radojković, (1966) pp. 126–7, 129.

108   Reliquary
1615
Cast silver; open-work, embossed, chased; silver-gilt
Height: 365 mm   Length: 375 mm   Width: 126 mm
Made for the monastery of Tvrdoš, Herzegovina.

In the form of a seven-domed church with narthex and apse. The
narthex is rectangular, with openings for three doors and two
windows. The roof of the narthex is lower than the roof of the
church, and it bears ornament of triangles executed by chiselling.
The apse is semicircular with a hemispherical roof, chiselled with
ornamented windows. A door is perforated between the narthex
and nave. Three ornamented windows are applied to either side
of the nave, which are also decorated with a frame of Gothic
trefoils. The roof has two sides. In the middle stand three domes
with Gothic hexagonal drums beginning with trefoils and continuing with rosettes. To the sides are two pairs of turrets with
rectangular bases. Above the drums rise cones with cross finials.
   This piece is a hybrid of Turkish and domestic elements, while
influenced by Venetian Gothic (vines with cross-shaped leaflets

and Gothic tambours) which also survived for a long time in the
workshops of Herzegovina.
   This reliquary was made under the influence of the architecture
of the time, being perhaps even a complete miniature of a real
church. The Turkish ornamentation on this piece is very finely
executed.
   The reliquary was made in 1615 for the monastery of Tvrdoš
by order of Simeon, the Metropolitan of Belgrade.

Treasury of the monastery of Savina
Literature: B. Radojković, (1966) pp. 128–9.

109   Reliquary
1617
Cast silver; open-work, chased
Height: 340 mm   Length: 220 mm   Width: 120 mm
Made for the monastery of Orakhovica, Slavonia.

A cubical box set on four stylized small legs, three of its sides with
apsidal projections, the fourth with a small door. The two-sided
roof carries three bigger and four smaller turrets. The reliquary is
decorated all over with tendrils, rosettes, birds and crosses. It is
engraved with an inscription referring to the Prior Hieromonk
Zachariah, who commissioned the piece, and the goldsmith
Avramije Hlapović, who made it.
   One of the best Herzegovinian craftsmen, Hlapović wrought a
whole series of objects for the Slavonian monastery of Orakhovica. Through these and other pieces of his one can trace the
evolution of this excellent master. All his works bear a Gothic
mark. In time, he developed an architectonic plan for his reliquaries and thus even suggested some solutions to the problems
of contemporary architecture.
   Often he used the same moulds for his articles, which makes
their attribution to him possible, even if the pieces are not signed
or marked.
   The vines and gables as well as other architectural solutions on
this reliquary reflect the late naturalistic phase of Gothic. This
style, cherished by the Herzegovinian workshops, was included
with Turkish motifs, contemporary architectural forms, and
Renaissance decorative elements.

The monastery of Orakhovica.
Literature: B. Radojković, (1966) pp. 127–8.

109

110 Reliquary
1705
Cast silver; open-work, wrought, embossed, chased; enamelled
Height: 420 mm   Length: 500 mm   Width: 270 mm
Made for the monastery of Ravanica, Mt. Fruška Gora, Serbia.

Composed of wrought plates divided into two belts and decorated with enamel, filigree and gilding. The lower belt is chased with figures of saints in arcades. Above are half-figures of saints: the Grand Duke St. Lazar, St. Sava and St. Simeon (the Serbian Saints); then St. Romil, St. Peter, St. John the Apostle, St. Andrew and St. Jacob; on the eastern side: St. Nicholas and St. Anastasius; on the northern side: St. Stephan, St. John the Eloquent, St. Gregory, St. Basileios, St. Luke, St. Mark, St. Matthew, and St. Paul. The Annunciation is represented on the portal. A large dome is set in the centre of the roof, with four smaller ones on the corners. A long inscription about the founder is on the door, with another inscription referring to the master builder on the eastern gable.

This reliquary is a copy of the Serbian Church of Ravanica with a *trichonkhos* at the base; stylistically, it belongs to the Moravska School (1371–1459). The monastery of Ravanica is dedicated to the Ascension, and the Ascension Day Hymn is inscribed on the reliquary. The place of honour given on it to the Serbian Saints is a reflexion of the socio-political situation prevailing after the Great Migration of the Serbs under the leadership of Arsenije Carnojević, in 1690.

Ciprovac, where the reliquary was made, was a great goldsmithing centre, and Nikola is one of the best-known masters from this centre.

The reliquary was ordered in 1705 and donated to the Monastery by the monk Leontes.

Museum of the Serbian Orthodox Church, Belgrade
Literature: B. Radojković, (1977) p. 149.

110

111 Reliquary

Delivered to the Monastery on 5th May, 1707
Cast silver; embossed; silver-gilt, enamelled
Height: 215 mm   Length: 180 mm
Made for the monastery of Krušedol, Mt. Fruška Gora.

In the form of a rectangular single-naved church with an apse and three domes, and set on four highly stylized lions. The west end is embossed with the Annunciation instead of a portal. Figures of Despot Jovan and Despot Stefan are in the arcades on the southern side, and the Despot's wife, Angelina, with the Bishop Maxim on the northern. The whole space around the figures is filled with enamel and there are birds on the columns. Three domes with circular drums decorated with filigree and enamel are set along the middle of the flat roof. The apse is semicircular, with a Turkish-style cupola and an inscription all over its surface.

This reliquary was made by Nikola Nedeljković after the model of the Ravanica reliquary of 1705; the artist even used the same moulds for some parts of it. The acrostic in the inscription says that this reliquary-artophorion was ordered by 'the one unworthy of sitting among the chosen ones,' in his desire that it might 'adorn the sacred family of the monastery of Krušedol...' It is signed by Avakum, the Prior of the monastery of Krušedol and the name of the artist is also mentioned in the inscription.

Museum of the Serbian Orthodox Church, Belgrade
Literature: Dr. Lazar Mirković, (1931) pp. 36–37; and R. Radoj-ković, (1966) pp. 149, 151.

Translated into English by
Aleksander Saša Petrović
Belgrade
1981

Bibliography

D. Milošević, *Medieval Art in Serbia*, Belgrade, 1969

D. Milošević, *Art in Medieval Serbia from the 12th to the 17th centuries*, Belgrade, 1980

L. Mirković, *The Antiquities of the monasteries of Fruška Gora*, Belgrade, 1931

B. Radojković, *Art-work in Metal*, Belgrade, 1956

B. Radojković, '16th and 17th century Serbian Gospel Mounts', *Zbornik of the Museum of Applied Art*, III–IV Belgrade, 1958

B. Radojković, 'The Turco-Persian influences on Serbian decorative arts of the 16th and 17th centuries,' *Zbornik Likovne umetnosti*, I, Novi Sad, 1965

B. Radojković, Some characteristics of Kotor's Goldsmiths' work and its influence on the Inland,' *The Antiquities of Montenegro*, III–IV, Cetinie, 1965–66

B. Radojković, *Serbian Goldsmiths' work of the 16th and 17th centuries*, Novi Sad, 1966

B. Radojković, *Jewellery in Serbia*, Belgrade, 1969

B. Radojković, 'Les métiers d'art dans la Serbie moravienne,' *Zbornik Filozofoskog fakulteta* (simpozijum: Moravska skola i njeno doba [The Moravian school and its era]), Belgrade, 1972

B. Radojković, 'The silver cups of Serbian origin from the necropolis of Bela Reka,' *Zbornik of the Museum of Applied Art*, XVI–XVII, Belgrade, 1972–3

B. Radojković, *Les objets sculptés d'art mineur en Serbie ancienne*, Belgrade, 1977

B. Radojković, 'Medieval Metalwork,' in, *The History of Applied Art in Serbia*, Belgrade, 1977

M. Šakota, *The Treasury of Banja Monastery*, Belgrade, 1981

M. Tatić, *Medieval Art in Serbia*, Belgrade, 1969

Glossary

Christ *Pantocrator* 'The Ruler of All'. Shown either seated or standing, the Gospels in the left hand, the right hand blessing.

Deisis A composition of Byzantine origin which shows Christ with Mary and St. John the Baptist on either side as mediators for mankind.

Mandorla A glory of light, usually elliptical in form, which completely surrounds a figure.

Metropolitan A bishop in Eastern churches ranking above an archbishop and below a patriarch.

Panagia 'The All Holy', i.e., the Virgin Mary.

Reliquary – artophorion A container, usually shaped as an aedicule or small church, which is used as a reliquary, or as a tabernacle for the Eucharist.

Ripidon (pl. ripida) A disc-shaped liturgical fan of metal on a handle, usually decorated with scenes from the Gospels.

Spakhia A potentate of military origin.

Stemategirion A garland or chaplet.

Tetraevangelion The four Gospels.

The Virgin
Eleusa 'The merciful'. The Mother of God holding the Infant Christ who rests his cheek on hers. Also known as the *Glykophilusa*.
Hodegetria The Mother of God bearing the Infant Christ on her left arm.
orans 'praying'. The mother of God is shown frontally with both hands raised in prayer.
Paraklesis The Mother of God stands in half profile, mostly to the R., with her further hand on her breast, and a scroll in her other, the text being a dialogue between Mother and Son in which she prays for mercy for mankind. This iconographical type was especially popular as an autonomous painting in Serbia.
Platytera Like the *orans* but with a half-figure of the Infant Christ shown in a medallion on her breast.